Structuring Schools for Success

Total Quality Education for the World's Best Schools

The Comprehensive Planning and Implementation Guide for School Administrators

Series Editor: **Larry E. Frase**

1 **The Quality Education Challenge**
   Carolyn J. Downey, Larry E. Frase, Jeffrey J. Peters

2 **Total Quality Education**
   Transforming Schools Into Learning Places
   Fenwick W. English, John C. Hill

3 **Creating Learning Places for Teachers, Too**
   Larry E. Frase, Sharon C. Conley

4 **The TQE Principal**
   A Transformed Leader
   Richard Sagor, Bruce G. Barnett

5 **Building Coalitions**
   How to Link TQE Schools With Government, Business, and Community
   Betty E. Steffy, Jane Clark Lindle

6 **Teacher Unions and TQE**
   Building Quality Labor Relations
   William A. Streshly, Todd A. DeMitchell

7 **Multiculturalism and TQE**
   Addressing Cultural Diversity in Schools
   Paula A. Cordeiro, Timothy G. Reagan, Linda P. Martinez

8 **Making Governance Work**
   TQE for School Boards
   William K. Poston Jr.

9 **TQE, Technology, and Teaching**
   Eugene R. Hertzke, Warren E. Olson

10 **Tools for Achieving TQE**
   Raymond F. Latta, Carolyn J. Downey

11 **Structuring Schools for Success**
   A View From the Inside
   Mary Scheetz, Tracy Benson

12 **Planning and Troubleshooting Guide**

The authors dedicate this series to the memory of
W. Edwards Deming, 1900-1993

Structuring Schools for Success

A View From the Inside

Mary Scheetz
Tracy Benson

CORWIN PRESS, INC.
A Sage Publications Company
Thousand Oaks, California

Copyright ©1994 by Corwin Press, Inc.

All rights reserved. No part of this book may be reproduced or utilized in any form or by any means, electronic or mechanical, including photocopying, recording, or by any information storage and retrieval system, without permission in writing from the publisher.

For information address:

Corwin Press, Inc.
A Sage Publications Company
2455 Teller Road
Thousand Oaks, California 91320

SAGE Publications Ltd.
6 Bonhill Street
London EC2A 4PU
United Kingdom

SAGE Publications India Pvt. Ltd.
M-32 Market
Greater Kailash I
New Delhi 110 048 India

Printed in the United States of America

Library of Congress Cataloging-in-Publication Data

Scheetz, Mary.
    Structuring schools for success: a view from the inside / Mary Scheetz, Tracy Benson.
       p. cm. — (Total quality education for the world's best schools, v. 11)
    Includes bibliographical references.
    ISBN 0-8039-6130-8 (pbk: alk. paper)
    1. School management and organization—United States—Case studies. 2. Total quality management—United States—Case studies. 3. Orange Grove Middle School (Tucson, Ariz.) I. Benson, Tracy. II. Title. III. Series.
LB2806.S3413 1994
371.2'009791'776—dc20   93-44471

94 95 96 97 98 10 9 8 7 6 5 4 3 2 1

Corwin Press Production Editor: Marie Louise Penchoen

Contents

Foreword	vii
Larry E. Frase	
Preface	ix
About the Authors	xv
1. Shifting Paradigms for Organizational Development	**1**
Shifting Paradigms	1
Interdependent Relationships	2
Personal Responsibility	6
Beyond Linear Thinking	8
Dealing With Dynamic Complexity	11
Key Terms and Concepts	14
Sources	14
Recommended Literature	15
2. Creating a Productive Environment	**16**
The Importance of a Well-Defined Culture	16
Developing Effective Communication Skills	17
Collaboration as a Way to Increase the Potential of a System	24
Community of Learners	28
Key Terms and Concepts	31
Sources	31
Recommended Literature	32
3. Exploring and Changing Mental Models	**33**
What are Mental Models?	33

Examining Existing Mental Models	35
Adopting New Mental Models as Necessary	41
Key Terms and Concepts	44
Source	44
Recommended Literature	45

4. Determining the Desired Results of the Organization — 46
Defining Desired Results — 46
Clarifying Personal Vision — 47
Evolution of a Shared Vision — 49
Clarifying Shared Vision — 51
Deriving Desired Results From a Shared Vision — 53
Key Terms and Concepts — 57
Source — 57
Recommended Literature — 57

5. Adjusting Organizational Structures — 58
Aligning Organizational Structures With Desired Results — 58
The Concept of Leverage — 61
The Concept of Feedback — 62
Structural Alignment — 66
Key Terms and Concepts — 73
Sources — 74
Recommended Literature — 74

6. Using Support Structures Outside of the School — 75
The Need for Outside Support Structures — 75
The District — 75
The Community — 77
Other Possibilities — 80
Key Terms and Concepts — 82
Sources — 83

7. Visualizing Next Steps — 84
Asking Essential Questions — 84
Successive Approximation — 85
Responses and Responsibilities — 86
Key Terms and Concepts — 88
Recommended Literature — 88

Planning and Troubleshooting Guide — 89

Foreword

This book offers the steps, methods, and strategies a team of professional educators successfully used in one school to develop Total Quality Education (TQE). The school is Orange Grove Middle School in the Catalina Foothills School District in Tucson, Arizona. The key strategies for accomplishing this success are spelled out in detail. Administrators, teachers, board members, and parents will find this account immensely helpful in integrating the many theories and practices provided by books in this series into one school's perspective.

Applying new educational theory is always easier to talk about than write about and certainly far easier than actually doing it. In this task, the authors were equal partners. Principal Mary Scheetz and Assistant Principal Tracy Benson were undaunted by this challenge and have designed and built a superior school based on TQE principles. They started with their well-founded ideas about creating a TQE middle school. Their ideas were immediately accepted and funded by private benefactors. Further, their work is held in such high esteem that Professor Emeritus Brown of the Massachusetts Institute of Technology has served as advisor to the project. The authors share their experiences in this book.

Important, current concepts covered include a shifting paradigm of organizational development, dynamic complexity of interpersonal relations and belief, mental models, shared visions, alignment of organizational structures, school structural changes, leverage, and successive approximation. With these concepts and the suggested procedures, readers can find a solid means of creating purposeful change. In this respect, it is a guidebook for developing a TQE school.

Larry E. Frase
San Diego State University

Preface

Designing an effective and efficient program for today's schools is a tremendous challenge. Confronted with the phenomenal growth of knowledge, innumerable academic study and career choices, and the changing values of our society, educators must combine their accumulated experience and training with the latest research to produce curriculum and instruction that will prepare students for future success. Implementing effective curriculum and instruction greatly depends on the ability of the organizational environment to balance traditional and innovative approaches and to maintain continual improvement in the face of increasing responsibility and decreasing financial support.

To implement changes in programs, school structures must accommodate the learning process for adults as well as students. New instructional practices require new organizational practices. Changing these practices requires applying what is known about the change process and about adult learning. Long-held beliefs and habits are deeply embedded in the ways that schools operate. Improving education involves determining which beliefs and habits are producing the results desired and which beliefs and habits should be changed. Educational leaders are faced with many questions.

- Where do we begin?
- How do we increase the potential for identifying effective change?

- How do we manage the transition to new ways of thinking and operating?
- What do we know that might be helpful in this transition?
- What might we learn from the business world that is facing the same need for change?

The contents of this book are based mainly on the experiences of the staff of Orange Grove Middle School in Tucson, Arizona. The school is located in the suburban Catalina Foothills School District. The district is growing rapidly and has expanded from one middle school to two middle schools, from three elementary schools to four elementary schools, and from a K-8 school district to a K-12 school district during the past 3 years.

The pace of change for Orange Grove Middle School has also been rapid. At the same time that plans for a transition from one junior high to two middle schools was being implemented, other projects were evolving. Those projects included curricular assessment and revision, instructional assessment and revision, and organizational assessment and revision. Over time it became obvious that the effectiveness of the organizational development was a key to the effectiveness of curriculum and instruction. A wide variety of resources and strategies were used to develop awareness, understanding, and skills that would maximize the potential of the school as a whole. The goal was to develop an organization that exemplified the concept of the whole being greater than the sum of the parts. In pursuing that goal, much was learned about individual and organizational thinking and behavior.

In chapter 1, "Shifting Paradigms for Organizational Development," the concept of managing improvement in schools is introduced. Traditionally, we have made changes in educational programs without addressing the paradigms (attitudes, beliefs, perceptions) that are necessary for the change. To further complicate the situation, the changes attempted were often the result of simplistic problem-solving strategies that ignored the complexity of the world of schools. Both students and adults can be taught to deal more effectively with dynamic, complex situations. This book focuses on the learning of the adults, specifically the members of a school staff.

Chapter 2, "Creating a Productive Environment," considers how the introduction of dynamic complexity can result in a sense of fear on the part of staff members. Dealing with dynamic complexity requires going beyond the isolated decision making and operational practices that are common in schools. It is not possible without effective communication and collaboration or without an understanding of each individual's purpose and importance in the organization. A culture in which communication, collaboration, and personal responsibility are expected necessitates the acquisition of new skills and new attitudes. Experiences designed to develop those skills and attitudes must be carefully planned and must include an assessment of current needs and readiness.

Chapter 3 is titled "Exploring and Changing Mental Models." To facilitate the evolution of a supportive environment that is conducive to communication, collaboration, and personal responsibility, it is necessary to determine the beliefs and assumptions that already exist in relationship to these and other values of the organization. Once these beliefs and assumptions have surfaced, the need for changes can be identified and strategies to bring about those changes can be planned. In most cases, the awareness of existing paradigms can be the most important first step toward necessary changes.

Chapter 4, "Determining the Desired Results of the Organization," explores how a vision can be developed as a result of exposing existing values. This process includes a recursive series of steps that leads to increasing clarification of personal visions and increased sharing of an organizational vision. Based on this somewhat abstract vision, desired results and more measurable, concrete outcomes can be identified.

Chapter 5, "Adjusting Organizational Structures," maintains that, if the vision is to be realized, the structures of the organization must be consistent with that vision. As with mental models, the existing structures should be analyzed to determine the degree of alignment with the vision. Once analyzed, the need for change can be assessed. It is possible that all structures might need adjustment. Attempting to make such massive change most often results in chaos and frustration. Determining the leverage in the situation—that is, the changes that are most likely to produce the results desired—includes carefully assessing current dynamics as well as potential consequences of change. Once structures have been designed and/or adjusted, the job has just begun. Feedback mechanisms must then be designed to provide information about results being produced. Through these feedback mechanisms, judgments about additional adjustments can be made. It is important to include a variety of opportunities for feedback in order to maximize the perspectives on the system. One source of tools for feedback is the total quality concept. Another is the field of system dynamics, which provides strategies for analyzing the interrelationships of a system and predicting the long-term results of changes made and actions taken within a system.

Chapter 6, "Using Support Structures Outside of the School," acknowledges that the challenge of developing a productive organization within a school is time-consuming and requires great effort and dedication. However, it is not enough to work only within the school. The school does not exist in isolation. Conditions within the school depend to a great extent on the support and understanding of several other groups including other schools, central administration, parents, and community. Working with and responding to the needs and actions of these other systems is crucial to the success of the school.

Chapter 7 addresses "Visualizing Next Steps." Publicity about the Orange Grove project has brought about a great deal of attention. Persons reading about and/or visiting the school tend to want to produce similar results in their own schools. Repeatedly, they ask "Where do we begin?" The answers to this question are varied. Each situation requires careful analysis and, ultimately, a process for planning and decision making. The process is recursive and may include analysis, decision making, and synthesis. These steps require patience and involve a certain degree of risk. However, it is the only way to make progress.

In these days of educational restructuring, ideas for improving schools abound. Many of these ideas do not address the interdependent relationships of the varied aspects of schooling. To increase the potential for success, we must synthesize to the greatest degree possible what we have learned from the past with what we know about present and future conditions. Efforts focused on this synthesis have resulted in an eclectic approach at Orange Grove Middle School. The strategies used there can benefit others who are struggling to design and implement plans for restructuring. It is with great humility that these strategies are proposed. No strategy or set of strategies will produce the same results in two different settings. Because the Orange Grove project has been in place for only 5 years, long-term results are yet to be determined. However, the initial results indicate much potential for the approaches to organizational development that have been adopted by the Orange Grove staff.

This book is an effort to share what has been learned and includes suggested procedures for implementing the concepts involved. These procedures are much like lesson plans that can be used to build staff awareness and skills. A basic premise is that educational leaders must see themselves as teachers who are responsible for the growth and learning of staff members. As awareness and skills are developed and practiced, the benefits of increased productivity can be realized. The suggested learning procedures range from facilitating staff members through the development of a shared vision to collaborative restructuring of the school to achieve the vision. Descriptions of risk factors and/or helpful hints are provided to increase the potential for successful use of the procedures. If approached from a teaching and learning standpoint, the strategies and activities proposed can be used, reused, adapted, and built on to fit the specific needs of any school.

Mary Scheetz
Tracy Benson
Orange Grove Middle School

About the Authors

Mary Scheetz is the Principal of Orange Grove Middle School in the Catalina Foothills School District in Tucson, Arizona. She has 23 years of experience in schools, including 5 years as a curriculum coordinator, 4 years as an assistant principal, and 6 years as a principal. She completed her master's degree at the University of Kansas. She has worked on several educational and community projects dedicated to the continual improvement of education. She has served as a speaker and/or consultant for many local, state, and national conferences, school districts, and university seminars.

Tracy Benson is the Assistant Principal of Orange Grove Middle School in the Catalina Foothills School District in Tucson, Arizona. She has 15 years of experience in schools, including 10 years of teaching, 2 years as a teacher evaluator and coach, and 3 years in school administration. She completed her undergraduate work at St. Lawrence University and her master's degree at Northern Arizona University. She has served as a speaker and/or consultant for state and national conferences, school districts, and university seminars.

*To the staff and students of Orange Grove Middle School,
Dr. Gordon Brown,
Jim and Faith Waters,
with gratitude, respect, and appreciation
for their dedication, efforts, and support*

✦ 1 ✦

Shifting Paradigms for Organizational Development

Shifting Paradigms

Historically, educational reform has been characterized by pendulum swings from one trend to another. Existing paradigms that involve a narrow focus on isolated symptoms of a problem tend to result in jumping from one short-term solution to another. We need to adopt a new paradigm that will result in more effective and longer-term solutions that truly address the causes of problems—not just the symptoms. The concepts and processes discussed in this book are based on the belief that the power to bring about effective change lies in the thinking of the individuals involved. Four basic shifts in the way we think are necessary to the new paradigm:

- From organizations operating in isolation with little regard for other parts of the organization to . . . *consideration of interdependence* (Kauffman, 1980)
- From dependence on compliance as a mode of operation to . . . *a goal of commitment and personal responsibility for the effects that actions have on other parts of the system* (Senge, 1990)
- From a linear view of X causes Y to . . . *a more complex systemic view of the variety of causal or influential relationships that exist in a school* (Goodman, 1991)

- From a focus on isolated or unrelated details to . . . *a practice of synthesizing information for a greater understanding of the complicated ways in which schools work* (Brown, 1992)

Interdependent Relationships

To manage a school, it is necessary to develop a perception of the school as a system, a collection of parts that interact with each other, to function as a whole (Kauffman, 1980). The world is a complex system "where all the subsystems overlap and affect each other. The common mistake is to deal with one subsystem in isolation, as if it didn't connect with anything else. This almost always backfires as other subsystems respond in unanticipated ways" (Kauffman, 1980, p. 38).

The concept of interdependence can be defined as the tendency for actions in one part of the system to affect other parts of the system. Pairs of interdependent subsystems in schools are easily identified: curriculum and instruction, staff development and staff evaluation, team groupings and department groupings, and so on. However, the overlaps extend far beyond these pairs and involve each subsystem's effect on every other subsystem and on the system as a whole.

During 1 week in a typical school, the following might happen:

- An eighth-grade assembly in the multipurpose room requires a special schedule and affects the classes on every other team.
- Purchasing materials for a new math program will greatly increase the effectiveness of math instruction but will use most of the building resources available for instructional materials.
- An innovative teacher plans a special unit based on attendance at a recent workshop and unknowingly purchases and uses instructional materials already being used in another subject.
- A grade-level team decides to implement a new disciplinary sequence without informing those who will be responsible for assigning the consequences.

- A group of teachers reaches a point of total frustration with a student and demands suspension only to learn that the counselor has been working with the student's dysfunctional family for several weeks.
- Teachers plan to use the student lunch area of the multipurpose building for a presentation by a speaker but do not meet with the custodian to discuss the work that will be necessary to have the area ready by the time it is needed.

One can easily conclude that everything is connected to everything else. This conclusion may be accurate but is only helpful if connections are analyzed and interventions are implemented. In each of the situations described above, the following questions should be asked:

- Who or what is affected by decisions, and what are the short- and long-term effects?
- What information is needed?
- What structures would facilitate communication?

These questions can be asked in relationship to a specific situation or as an analysis of the entire system with follow-up planning.

The following suggested procedures will assist the school leader in understanding the interdependent nature of school systems. Suggested Procedure 1 provides a framework for structuring a school system into interdependent subsystems. Suggested Procedure 2 provides an exercise that can help the school administrator facilitate the exploration of interdependence with the school staff. To assure that all perspectives are considered, the following activities are most successful if all staff members are involved.

Suggested Procedure 1: Creating Interdependent Structures

Assuming that the primary goal of an organization is to increase the effectiveness and efficiency of the total system, there is a need to break that system into manageable subsystems with common focuses or purposes. These subsystems or teams work together toward their common purpose and continue to function as a part of the whole system. Teams are expected to maintain the

4 ✧ Structuring Schools for Success

understanding of the relationship of their part to others within the system and also to the whole by timely communication, awareness, and by addressing common concerns. Examples of teams in a school setting include the following:

> Grade-level teams: interdisciplinary focus (i.e., fifth-grade teachers)
>
> Department teams: curriculum focus (i.e., middle school science teachers)
>
> Services teams: focus on serving all staff/programs (i.e., librarians, custodians, secretaries, counselors, nurses, administrators, etc.)
>
> Support teams: focus on students with special needs (i.e., special educators, gifted educators, psychologists, etc.)

Suggested Procedure 2: Analyzing the System's Ability to Address Interdependencies

> Step 1: Identify and describe the existing communication/collaboration structures that exist in the system (examples: department meetings, staff development committees, memos, computerized mail, etc.).
>
> Step 2: Determine the needs that are not being addressed (examples: custodial staff consistently uninformed and not included in decision making/planning, teachers of special classes are not considered in plans for schedule changes, budget decisions do not address the needs of the whole system, etc.).
>
> Step 3: Decide if new structures are necessary or if use of existing structures should be changed.
>
> Step 4: Design new structures or new practices for existing structures (examples: Every staff member is assigned to a team, task groups for major issues include a representative from every team, copies of team minutes are sent to every other team, support personnel meet with each team on a regular basis, etc.).

Step 5: Implement new structures and practices.
Step 6: Monitor and adjust as necessary.
Step 7: Return to Step 1 on a regular basis.

RISK FACTOR

Identifying needs is the easy part. Examining existing structures and practices can be threatening. First attempts to implement this process should be depersonalized and blameless. The activity can be made safer by using (a) small groups, (b) written responses rather than discussion, (c) generic situations rather than real-world situations, (d) and first-person (I, we) rather than third-person (you, they) pronouns.

HELPFUL HINT 1

"The road to success is always under construction" (Anonymous). It is better to take carefully planned initial steps and to continuously assess progress before planning next steps. Just as classroom teachers are asked to assess readiness, so must administrators assess the readiness of staff members for each and every organizational development task. To proceed too quickly, to take steps that are too big, or to ask too much too soon will result in a loss of trust and confidence and will make further progress more difficult.

HELPFUL HINT 2

A variety of resource materials based on the concept of interdependence and the skills necessary to deal with interdependence are available. Books can be introduced through a book talk in the library. Minilessons can be developed by staff members who have read materials or attended workshops. Discussions about ideas and potential uses can be held. Whatever resources are used, it is important to establish an environment that supports staff learning and sharing of information. Resources that have been used at Orange Grove Middle School are referenced in this book.

Personal Responsibility

An essential component when dealing with interdependence is developing a sense of personal responsibility within each and every staff member within the school community. Common questions that are helpful in determining the degree to which individuals take personal responsibility for their behaviors, decisions, and attitudes include the following:

- What responsibilities do individuals or groups have for communicating and/or working with others?
- What attitudes about personal responsibility are necessary?
- Are behaviors consistent with the attitudes and responsibilities that have been identified?

Helping each staff member to build the habits of personal responsibility for the whole system is a major challenge. In most schools the need to take care of one's own priorities first has been reinforced. Efforts to maximize some subsystems at the expense of others or at the expense of the system as a whole have been accepted. "What supplies or materials can I get for *my* classroom?" "What workshops and in-services will benefit *my* teaching?" "How much time do I need to plan *my* program?" In a time when resources are scarce, it is more common to "get as much as you can" rather than working together to determine the most effective use of what is available. Traditional structures within schools create or perpetuate isolation. While working in isolation it is difficult to feel any sense of responsibility for other parts of the system. Yet that is exactly what staff members must do if we are to effectively deal with interdependencies.

The following suggested procedure is a problem-solving exercise that helps individuals look at a variety of situations from different perspectives. By understanding different perspectives, individuals can develop a sense of personal responsibility for the system as a whole.

*Suggested Procedure: Open-Mindedness Exercise
(adapted from Synectics, Inc.)*

>Step 1: Assign individuals to work together in pairs. Designate one individual as first person, the other as second person.
>
>Step 2: Assign the first person to give a brief overview of a problem or opportunity that he or she is dealing with and a brief (2 to 3 minutes) summary of background information, including the following:
>a. Why is this a problem or opportunity?
>b. Why is it his or her responsibility?
>c. What has already been tried or thought of?
>d. What is wanted ideally from this meeting?
>Assign the second person to listen, trying to get a feeling for the first person's wishes and concerns in the matter. In the interest of time, do not allow further clarification unless absolutely necessary.
>
>Step 3: Assign the second person to take a moment to think of a suggestion that is novel—that is, it represents, as far as is known, a departure from the present way of doing things. The suggestion should be offered to the first person.
>
>Step 4: Assign the first person to paraphrase or state understanding of the suggestion until the second person agrees that it is understood. The second person is not allowed to repeat the suggestion until it has been paraphrased. Assign the second person, if necessary, to restate part of the idea that was left out or misunderstood.
>
>Step 5: Assign the first person to give three pluses (potential advantages, useful implications of the suggestions), then key concerns in order of importance and in "how-to" form. Instruct the second person to resist temptation to "help out" the first person by suggesting pluses for the suggestion, but allow him or her to offer both pluses and concerns after the first person has completed his or her response.

Step 6: Assign the entire group to spend a moment reflecting on the process. Ask them to consider the types of responsibilities that they felt as they talked, listened, suggested, responded, and so on.

Step 7: Ask for group feedback based on their reflection. Ask some form of the following questions:
  a. Is it helpful to understand another person's situation?
  b. Did they learn about similarities or differences?
  c. Is it helpful to receive suggestions from others?
  d. Is it helpful to acquire a new perspective?
  e. How might this or similar exercises be used to help all staff members take personal responsibility for helping others or to take the personal responsibility to listen to the suggestions of others?

Beyond Linear Thinking

The world is often perceived as operating in a linear, sequential cause-effect manner. The focus is on events. The desire for solutions to produce immediate effects is evident. People assume that some influence outside of their control is creating their problems. When things are different than planned, there is a need to assign blame and fault, which is focused and specific. Scapegoats are rampant, necessary, and popular. Much time and effort is dedicated to finding a final right answer.

School planning often results from analytical, linear problem solving. The format of the plans usually includes sequential steps that are implemented in the order proposed with little or no consideration of the results that are produced by each step and little or no adjustment based on feedback. The steps of the plan become a list of events that can be checked off when completed. If the plan fails, many external influences are available for blame.

To improve both the plans and the implementation of the plans, staff members must be taught to look at the "big picture," to use synthesis in addition to analysis. It is necessary to understand that each action creates new sets of conditions, new interrelationships that must be addressed. Procedures for monitoring and adjusting must be devised and used. Existing conditions and changes in conditions must be addressed.

The following processes are suggested for staff members as they practice a more systemic approach to implementing new strategies. Suggested Procedure 1 helps staff members recognize and understand the difference between linear and systemic thinking. Suggested Procedure 2 enables staff members to practice the skills of analysis and synthesis in addressing common concerns in schools.

Suggested Procedure 1: Practicing a New View of an Old Problem

When discussing educational innovations that have not worked, people often mention "new math." Educators and noneducators alike can list the mistakes that were made in the planning and implementation of this strategy. In most schools, staff members can describe other situations in which linear, nonsystemic thinking brought about negative results.

Step 1: Assign staff members to groups of three to four with one member of each grouping having had experience as a student or a teacher during the implementation of educational innovation that is known to have failed. Examples: new math, team/turn teaching, open classrooms.

Step 2: Assign each group to list (to the best of their knowledge) the steps that took place in the planning for, the implementation of, and the ultimate demise of new math.

Step 3: Have groups share their descriptions of what they believe to have happened.

Step 4: Assign each group to synthesize what they know about curriculum development, implementation, and human nature and to describe the following:
a. Desired conditions for effective implementation of curricular or instructional innovation

> b. Actions that are likely to produce those conditions
> c. Actions that are necessary to maintain those conditions
> d. Changes in conditions that are likely to take place as the innovation is implemented
>
> Step 5: Assign each group to design a process that includes procedures for actions prior to implementation, during implementation, and following implementation.
>
> Step 6: Each group shares their plans.
>
> Step 7: Process questions.

Possible other steps: Decision-making process to choose one of the ideas or to combine two or more to form a new process that will be implemented.

Suggested Procedure 2: The Big Questions (analysis and synthesis)

During the spring semester, each staff member is asked to list the three questions that most need to be addressed before the coming school year. It is possible to pose this as a totally open-ended question or to provide some introductory information that will lead the responders to focus on certain program areas or topics.

> Step 1: Obtain input from each staff member. What are the big questions that need to be answered as we prepare for next year?
>
> Step 2: Synthesize input and immediate responses where possible.
>
> Step 3: Meet with team representatives to discuss questions and/or responses.
>
> Step 4: Develop plans based on synthesis presented to staff members for reaction.
>
> Step 5: Finalize plans.
>
> Step 6: Implement plans.

Step 7: Analyze results on a continual basis, making adjustments as necessary.

Step 8: Return to Step 1 on a regular basis.

RISK FACTORS

For some people, there is a sense of safety in linear thinking. It appears logical and manageable and is easily defined. Moving into the realm of probability, of predicting changes, of addressing the complexities of human interaction can be threatening. It is certain to be frustrating because there are no definite, right answers. It is important to prepare for and to deal with this frustration. The struggle with the change in thinking should be validated. Support for the efforts to get through this struggle should be provided.

HELPFUL HINT

The use of style delineators can be helpful to staff members in increasing their understanding of themselves and of others. Information gained from the style delineator activities can also be used to determine which staff members might experience more difficulty with the ambiguity of the processes suggested above. It is essential that the various styles of staff members be valued and addressed in much the same way that teachers are expected to value and address the diverse styles that are represented in the classroom.

Dealing With Dynamic Complexity

Whether or not one views the current situation in education as a crisis, it is certainly obvious that problems exist and that the system is not producing satisfying results. Most solutions currently being proposed tend to address isolated details and suggest that quick fixes are possible. Such solutions do not address the dynamic complexity of the educational system.

Dynamic complexity exists in situations where cause and effect are subtle, and where the effects over time of interventions are not obvious. For example, the relationships between the causes and effects of student behavior are subtle and often elusive. Increased discipline problems during lunchtime may not truly be the result of ill-mannered students. In addressing the dynamic complexity of the situation, many other factors should be considered. Examples include the lack of activities or opportunities that students have to exert energy or relieve stress or pursue interests during their lunchtime, the length of the lunchtime, what students experience before their lunch, or rapport with lunch supervisors.

When the same action has dramatically different effects in the short run than in the long run, there is dynamic complexity. As schools begin to increase their capacity to purchase and implement technology, decisions need to be made about how to spend the budgeted monies. To spend a budgeted amount on hardware without planning for software, maintenance, networking, and training needs is an example of attending to the details and not the dynamics of a complex situation. Without attention to the dynamics of increased technological hardware in a school site, the long-term effects are easily predictable—computers that are seldom used.

When an action has one set of consequences locally and a very different set of consequences in another part of the system, there is dynamic complexity. A timely example is the implementation of site-based management. Different management styles will oftentimes produce different results. When staff members come together from sites that are managed with different sets of standards, practices, expectations, and procedures, frustration may result and conflicts can occur.

Although increasing individual and group ability to deal with dynamic complexity is crucial to the effectiveness of any organization, little is known about the methodologies for deducing the dynamics of social systems. Whatever methodology is chosen, its effectiveness will be increased if individuals have the awareness and skills necessary to understand dynamic complexity.

The following suggested procedure will (a) provide a process for designing staff development, (b) recommend specific skills necessary for understanding dynamic complexity, and (c) pose pertinent questions that will assist in the management of the dynamics evident in schools.

Suggested Procedure: Staff Development Design

Designing a continuous, recursive process of staff development activities that models an awareness of the dynamics existing in the school (levels of skills, types of training and experience, attitudes, habits, etc.) is difficult but necessary. The process should include activities that focus on the needs of both individuals and groups. Possible topics are innumerable but should include effective communication, understanding self and others, analyzing problem situations, predicting short- and long-term consequences of actions, observation, and inquiry. These topics assist staff members in developing the skills necessary to deal with complex situations and the challenges of the change process.

Management of organizational growth and development requires an understanding and consideration of the complexity and the ever-changing nature of the world of education. As plans are designed and decisions are made, the following questions assist in the management of the dynamics evident in schools:

- What long-term effects might result from this decision or action?
- Who will be affected by this decision or action?
- Who needs to have input in this decision?
- What are the potential benefits and possible trade-offs of this decision?
- What are the time constraints for making this decision?
- Who needs to understand the rationale for this decision?
- What support will be necessary for successful implementation?
- What attitudes or behaviors might contribute to the success of this plan?
- What attitudes or behaviors might inhibit the success of this plan?
- How can contributing attitudes and behaviors be enhanced?

A new view of management results when school leaders work to create environments where staff members gain new perspectives, think systemically, and recognize the complex effects of actions and decisions. The following chapter will discuss the importance of the school environment as one works to improve schools.

Key Terms and Concepts

Dynamic complexity. Situations where cause and effect are subtle, effects over time are not obvious, effects in different situations vary.

Dynamics. Patterns of change or growth, variations of behavior or intensity of behavior.

Interdependence. A combination of interrelationships that is not linear. The interrelationships are dependent on one another.

Linear thinking. Simple, sequential causality.

Paradigm. A conceptual framework or model. In work situations, commonly held paradigms lead to the establishment of accepted policies and procedures.

Style delineators. Tools such as the Meyers-Briggs, the Gregorc, 4-MAT, or True Colors that help individuals to classify their preferences and behaviors into categories.

Sources

Brown, G. S. (1992). Improving education in public schools: Innovative teachers to the rescue. *Systems Dynamics Review, 8*(1), 83-89.

Goodman, M. (1991). Systems thinking as a language. *The Systems Thinker, 2*(3), 3-4.

Kauffman, D. L., Jr. (1980). *Systems one: An introduction to systems thinking.* Minneapolis, MN: S. A. Carlton.

Senge, P. (1990). *The fifth discipline: The art and practice of the learning organization.* New York: Doubleday.

Recommended Literature

Draper, F. (1993). A proposed sequence for developing systems thinking in a grades 4-12 curriculum. In G. Richardson (Ed.), *Systems dynamics review* (pp. 207-214). New York: John Wiley.

Draper, F., & Swanson, M. (1990). Learner-directed systems education: A successful example. In G. Richardson (Ed.), *System dynamics review* (pp. 209-213). New York: John Wiley.

Forrester, J. W. (1969). *Principles of systems: Text and workbook.* Cambridge, MA: Productivity Press.

Meadows, D. H. (1991). *The global citizen.* Washington, DC: Island Press.

Orange Grove Middle School. (Producer). (1991). *New vision: Systems thinking in education.* [Videotape]. Tucson, AZ: Author.

Patterson, J. L., Purkey, S. C., & Parker, J. V. (1986). *Productive school systems for a nonrational world.* Alexandria, VA: Association for Supervision and Curriculum Development.

Richmond, B. (1990). *Systems thinking: A critical set of critical thinking skills for the 90's and beyond.* Paper written for High Performance Systems, Inc.

Synectics problem solving workshop. (1989). Cambridge, MA: Synectics.

Wycoff, J. (1991). *Mindmapping—Your personal guide to exploring creativity and problem-solving.* New York: Berkley Books.

✧ 2 ✧

Creating a Productive Environment

The Importance of a Well-defined Culture

Just as the farmer carefully prepares the soil in readiness for planting to ensure the proper environment for flourishing crops, organizations must prepare and nurture the environment for growth and productivity. The environment is more than the buildings, grounds, supplies, and furniture; it is the values, beliefs, traditions, and attitudes of the individuals who make up the organization. Those important environmental ingredients that members have in common can be described as the organizational culture. "A culture is a system of attitudes, actions, and artifacts that endures over time and that operates to produce among its members a relatively unique common psychology" (Vaill, 1989, p. 147).

When an organization develops a well-defined culture, members of the organization can consistently describe the essential aspects of the culture. Their behaviors and interactions are aligned with their descriptions. This alignment builds the foundation for organizational productivity and satisfaction in the workplace.

Where does one start? Like the farmer assessing the soil before planting, it is necessary to first examine the current status of the school environment. Climate surveys, observation, and individual and small-group conferences can be used for initial assessments. These formal and informal assessments will help formulate a clear picture of the existing culture. Questions that may be helpful in this initial assessment include the following:

- What are the impressions of guests who visit your campus?
- Do staff members talk about their work? What do they say?
- What are the topics of conversation in the staff lounge or work areas?
- What are the observable, consistent ways in which staff members behave that contribute to productivity?
- Are there inconsistencies in the ways staff members behave that become barriers to productivity?

A safe process where individuals share openly and feel they can trust will result in honest impressions and accurate information. Staff members should feel comfortable and encouraged to voice concerns, opinions, and ideas. Individuals should not worry about who may disagree or what may result from speaking up. The staff lounge should no longer be the hub of gossip and idle conversation. Up-front, honest, and respectful communication should be valued and reinforced consistently, therefore minimizing the need for secrecy and closed-door chatter.

The creation and preservation of a well-defined culture requires that the administrator(s) or leaders of the school operate as *teachers* in the design and implementation of learning opportunities for all staff. As teachers, they must engage in careful planning for the individual needs and development of all staff members. This will increase the effectiveness of formal and informal training opportunities. Those opportunities need to be meaningful; related to real and necessary tasks; and should involve staff members in design, implementation, and follow-up phases. To prepare for this process, all staff members should have a common language and opportunity for effective communication training.

Developing Effective Communication Skills

We live in an age of information overload where people are giving and receiving information through a variety of technologies. When there is less of a need for interpersonal communication, people are less likely to develop and value the benefits gained from face-to-face, old-fashioned dialogues. Today, we may talk to one another, but is communication really occurring?

Increasing understanding is the ultimate goal of communication. "If communication improves the quality of the relationship between two or more people, we must judge it from an overall standpoint to be effective" (Peck, 1987, p. 257). The purpose of communication is to remove the barriers of ignorance and/or misunderstanding. This may be accomplished by giving or receiving information (in writing, orally, or nonverbally), by seeking to understand the opinion of another, by recognizing similarities and differences in perspectives, or by participating in a meaningful exchange of ideas in order to create new and innovative approaches. All of these examples are necessary communication tasks that contribute to a learning, productive, and thriving organization.

In educational systems, communication has been labeled as a focus for growth, a blame for dysfunction, and a goal for the strategic plan. Because communication as an interpersonal skill cannot be mastered by reading a text or by attending a workshop, we need to have opportunities for learning and practicing essential communication skills.

The following skills have been identified as specific areas of communication that should prove helpful in the planning for staff training and development.

Dialogue. In dialogue, individuals seek to go beyond their own understanding. All points of view are shared for the purpose of seeing the "big picture." The goal of dialogue is to have each person understand different perspectives on a situation versus individuals lobbying for a side or an opinion. The assumption is that the whole (big picture) is greater than the sum of its parts (individual points of view). In his book *Unfolding Meaning,* David Bohm (1985) asserts,

> A new kind of mind thus begins to come into being which is based on the development of a common meaning that is constantly transforming in the process of dialogue. People are no longer primarily in opposition, nor can they said to be interacting, rather they are participating in this pool of common meaning, which is capable of constant development and change. (p. 141)

Discussion. The purpose of discussion is to share points of view on a subject in order to formulate one single view. Individuals may adjust their opinions based on what they have heard. The goal of discussion is to have a single view accepted by all, which can often result in a "win-lose" situation. The assumption is that some existing point of view will prevail.

As to the significance and usefulness of dialogue and discussion, Peter Senge (1990) in his book *The Fifth Discipline* contends that "both (dialogue and discussion) are important to a team capable of continual generative learning, but the power lies in their synergy, which is not likely to be present when the distinctions between them are not appreciated" (p. 240)

Active Listening. The active listener takes equal responsibility in effective communication. The listener does this by appropriately responding, questioning, paraphrasing, and providing nonverbal cues that are genuine and respectful.

Communication Under Stress. Effective communication skills become more difficult to practice when dealing with difficult or stressful situations. Understanding how different people react and respond in times of conflict or pressure and having opportunities to learn strategies for dealing with these situations is essential to maintaining a safe and productive work environment.

The following two suggested procedures will help the school leader reinforce the necessary effective communication skills for building a productive school environment. The first is a role-play simulation that deals with a common decision-making dilemma. The second uses the communication stances of Virginia Satir (1976) in an activity that helps to provide an increased awareness of how individuals communicate when under stress.

Suggested Procedure 1: A Principal's Dilemma

This simulation requires individuals to role-play a difficult decision-making session. This activity can facilitate a practice session in the communication skills of dialogue, discussion, and active listening.

THE SCENARIO

The ABC school received a new color-monitor computer as a gift from a local business. Gabriel Hernandez, the principal, needs to decide who should get the new computer. The following are some facts about some ABC staff members:

- Sandy: 17 years as the school's secretary; has a 5-year-old computer
- Leslie: 11 years as an English teacher; has a personally-owned computer in the classroom
- Pat: 10 years as the athletic director; has no computer
- Shawn: 5 years as the assistant principal; shares a computer with the principal
- Lee: 3 years as the computer teacher; oversees the school computer lab

THE ROLES

Gabriel Hernandez, Principal. In the past, there have often been hard feelings when new technology was allocated. Many members of the staff felt that they were entitled to the new equipment, so you had a tough time making a fair decision. As a matter of fact, it usually turned out that whatever you decided, most of the staff considered it wrong. To handle the current situation, you have decided to give the problem to a small representative group of the staff and ask them to decide what would be the fairest way to allocate the new computer. Your job will be to facilitate their discussion.

Sandy. You deserve the new computer because you have been with the school longer than any of the other staff members. As the school secretary, you obviously need the latest in technology as you keep track of student records, publish the school newsletter, and type all school correspondence. You would be perfectly willing to give your older computer away and provide training on its use.

Leslie. It is certainly your turn to receive the new computer. You have brought your own computer from home into your classroom because you feel it is essential for students to edit and publish their writing on computer. You have spent much of your own time and money training yourself in various software programs. You are considered the "computer wiz" of the school. You should also get the computer because you believe the business who donated the computer wanted it to assist student learning—so it should surely go in the classroom.

Pat. As the athletic director, you have to have a computer. Your athletic budget, schedule, inventory, and correspondence are all done by hand, and you do not even have a secretary. A strong athletic tradition has always been an important part of the success of the ABC school. Presently, all of the other schools you compete with have computerized athletic departments. Let us make sure we do not have a disadvantage off the field! After all, you also play golf with the CEO of the business who donated the computer.

Shawn. As the assistant principal, you are such a hard worker and spend many, many hours supervising after school and during evening activities. You have been sharing a computer with the principal, but it is very difficult to use the computer during the school day. The principal is often having meetings and talking on the phone during the time you need to use the computer. Because you are out supervising activities after school and during the evenings, you have little time to write memos, establish a discipline database, and check student records. Lately, you have been coming in on Saturdays and Sundays to get your work done on the computer. You deserve to have your own.

Lee. It is so obvious that the new computer belongs in the computer lab! Anyone can sign up to use it because you will set up a schedule for all staff members. As the computer technician, it is also important that you have immediate access to the new computer because it is your job to stay current with technology.

> Step 1: Assign each of the six roles; in small groups, role-play the problem. Ask groups to make a decision in the allotted time (20-30 minutes).

Step 2: Write down the results of each small group on a board or chart paper.

Step 3: In a large group, process the activity by asking the following questions:
  a. How did your group arrive at a decision?
  b. How did your group work together?
  c. What went well? What could have gone better?
  d. Did you feel listened to? Were your opinions valued?

Step 4: After a brief explanation of dialogue and discussion, ask the following questions:
  a. What technique did your group use more—dialogue or discussion?
  b. If you could do this activity again, what would you do differently?

HELPFUL HINTS

All staff members should be involved with training in effective communication. This will provide a common language and shared expectations, demonstrating that all members of the staff are essential and valued members of the organization.

RISK FACTORS

This activity may be sensitive depending on how close the scenario is to situations currently existing in your school. You can also present a generic situation unrelated to education as a safer topic for a group decision. It is important to determine the readiness of staff members by assessing their communication skills and the existing levels of trust as plans are created for staff training.

Suggested Procedure 2: Virginia Satir's Communication Stances

This activity has been extremely helpful for staff members as they examine the ways in which they communicate when faced with difficult situations. It also heightens awareness and understanding of why others react the way they do when under stress. Satir suggests four communication stances when individuals are faced with difficult situations: placating, blaming, superreasonableness, and irrelevance. This information can be taught in a variety of ways, and the following format is just one suggestion that has worked well with school staffs.

> Step 1: As the first stance is described (placating), ask a volunteer to assume a physical pose that would represent the description.
>
> Step 2: Ask for a second volunteer, and have the individual stand in close proximity to the "placating volunteer." Describe the blaming stance as the second volunteer assumes a "blaming" pose.
>
> Step 3: Ask for a third volunteer, again have the individual stand near the first two volunteers and describe the "superreasonableness" stance as the volunteer poses.
>
> Step 4: Ask for a final volunteer as the first three, describe "irrelevance," and ask the individual to pose. (All four volunteers should be physically representing their stances in close proximity to one another.)
>
> Step 5: Beginning with placating, ask each individual the following questions:
> a. What are you feeling?
> b. What are you trying to inspire in others?
> c. What feelings are you most likely wanting to avoid?
> d. What physical symptoms are you experiencing?
>
> Step 6: Thank the volunteers and now ask all staff members to reflect on a time when they were faced with a stressful situation. Ask them to stand and face a person with whom they feel comfortable and assume the stance that they most likely take when dealing with difficult situations.
>
> Step 7: Go through the same questions listed in Step 5 and ask the individuals to share their answers with their partners.
>
> Step 8: In small groups, ask individuals to share the stance they think they take most often. (Reinforce the point that sharing is voluntary.)
>
> Step 9: In large groups, ask individuals the following questions:
> a. What did you learn through this activity?
> b. How did you feel during this activity?

c. The next time you are in a stressful situation, what might you think about?
d. What thoughts or insights will you take with you today?

HELPFUL HINTS

When individuals feel uncomfortable, they often joke and make fun as they participate in the activity. When choosing volunteers, it may be helpful to ask individuals who you know will be appropriate models ahead of time to help the rest of the group take the activity seriously. Although laughter and a little silliness is to be expected, the exercise will only be effective if each individual truly recognizes and appreciates the stances of communication.

RISK FACTORS

Sometimes, when individuals learn new things about themselves, these can appear unsettling. Scheduling some downtime or a break right after the activity to "check in" with specific individuals is helpful and oftentimes necessary.

Collaboration as a Way to Increase the Potential of a System

"The ability to work well with others grows out of the qualities that contribute to healthy living: stability, honesty, clarity, inner confidence, and well-focused awareness" (Tulku, 1978, p. 113). When individuals are contributing their talents, skills, experiences, energies, and ideas within a team structure, the effectiveness of the sum of each individual is increased as a result of the whole. Within a collaborative team structure, which is supportive and trusting, people are more likely to

1. Take risks
2. Have the courage to be less than perfect
3. Accept the differences in others
4. Share responsibility
5. Seek the thoughts, ideas, and opinions of others

6. Be intrinsically motivated
7. Reflect on their own strengths and weaknesses
8. Strive for personal growth
9. Find satisfaction in the workplace

Effective collaboration includes an individual's ability to communicate and a personal willingness to see the value of being a member of a team or group versus working in isolation. As reported in the Secretary's Commission on Achieving Necessary Skills (SCANS) 1992 report, we understand that the ability to work well with others as a member of a team is considered a requisite skill for individuals entering the working world. Valuing and appreciating the skills needed to successfully work together is not enough. Collaboration and teaming are not easy concepts to implement. As educators, we need to learn, practice, and model collaboration. Carefully planned and sequenced tasks that help to facilitate team building and team collaboration should encourage the development of productive, effective, and supportive collaborative teams.

The following activities will help the school leader facilitate team building and team collaboration with newly formed teams of staff members. A sequence of learning activities for newly formed groups have been beneficial in helping individuals learn, practice, and develop collaborative skills. This sequence includes the following activities:

- Team building activities
- Team tasks (low to high risk)
- Reflection and assessment activities

As teams have increased opportunities to work with one another, the risk level of the activities can also be carefully increased. However, time should not be the only factor when determining the level of risk of activities and team tasks. Skill and trust levels should be important factors when planning. Activities and tasks of varying levels of risk are included in the activities in the following suggested procedures.

Suggested Procedure 1: Team Building

THE HUMAN KNOT ACTIVITY

This activity is a low-risk, goal-oriented team-building activity.

Step 1: In groups of 15 to 20, ask individuals to cluster together in a circle, put both hands in the center of the circle, and connect their hands with hands of two different people creating a large, tangled knot.

Step 2: As a group, try to untangle the human knot without releasing any connection.

Step 3: As groups work, provide encouragement and adequate time for them to accomplish the task.

Step 4: Ask individuals the following processing questions:
   a. What did your group do to accomplish the task?
   b. What strategies worked best in your group?
   c. What barriers were getting in the way of your group accomplishing the task?
   d. What comparisons can you draw from your experiences with this activity and real-life situations?

RISK FACTORS

Small groups can usually accomplish the task by successfully untangling their knot. On occasion, groups may have difficulty because of physical differences and limitations of some individuals. Before groups begin, you may want to offer a "disconnection coupon" to each group to help ensure that they succeed. Groups can then make one disconnection and reconnection during the activity.

Suggested Procedure 2: Team Tasks

These are examples of team tasks of varying risk. The following should be assigned based on the team's readiness to successfully accomplish each task:

- Determine what roles are needed on a team (low risk).
- Determine who assumes each role (medium to high risk).

- Determine when and where the team meets (low to medium risk).
- Determine communication structures within the team (low risk).
- Determine communication structures with other teams in the system (low risk).
- Decide on meeting format, guidelines, and procedures (medium risk).
- Determine how team decisions will be made (medium risk).
- Determine how the team budget will be managed (medium to high risk).
- Decide a procedure for adjusting the schedule for special programs or assemblies (medium risk).

RISK FACTORS

Depending on the nature of individuals on each team within the system, the level of trust, and the level of communication and collaborative skills, the above risk factors may be adjusted. Monitor the team process carefully in order to appropriately sequence the assignment of tasks.

Suggested Procedure 3: Reflection and Assessment

After teams have had a chance to work together, ask them to reflect and assess their effectiveness. This should be done with groups working privately. Only when a team is having serious problems should a nonteam facilitator be used. The following questions may be helpful in getting them started in this process. These can be answered in writing (low risk) or by using an open dialogue (medium to high risk) to share viewpoints.

- What strengths do you see in your team up to this point?
- What team event or occurrence stands out as being the most positive and/or productive?
- What one thing could you do personally that would help the team function more effectively?
- What outside support would help your team to continue to work productively?

RISK FACTORS

In beginning stages, it is important to ask questions in positive terms, and not those that could cause individuals to attack, defend, or blame themselves or others on their team. Focusing on the positive will increase the chances that teams will continue effective practices and supportive relationships. It may also be helpful to provide individuals with a set of questions before they are expected to write or share impressions. This will support individuals who work better when they are provided with adequate time to reflect and will result in more thoughtful responses. More concrete, outcome-based assessments can be reserved for more sophisticated teams who have had a variety of experiences to work through.

Community of Learners

Lifelong learner is a term that describes the individual who strives to question, seeks new understanding, masters new skills, and strives to perfect old skills as a lifelong mission. The term is found in many school mission statements and is a goal that many support. A staff of individuals who adopt this mission as a value and practice and as a model for students is exciting and influential.

This staff takes risks for the sake of learning. The importance of taking risks as a learner is in the discovery that one's potential can truly appear limitless. There is satisfaction working in an environment where there is little fear of failure because of the high priority and value placed on learning by one's mistakes. This is not to say that failure is nonexistent, but it is diminished by individuals gradually moving step-by-step toward success as defined by the desired result or goal. In an environment such as this, one finds that because the focus is on quality learning, individuals risk with more planning, more thoughtfulness, and more expertise. Thus the expectations for performance are not diminished; to the contrary, performance goes above basic expectations because individuals take advantage of opportunities to innovate and strive toward their limitless potentials.

The staff as a learning community develops a sense of collegiality because learning becomes a public and social process. Peer study groups, dialogue sessions, conflict resolution sessions, and collaborative teams are structures that contribute to the development of collegiality. Seeing one another as colleagues does not necessarily mean that all agree or all share the same point of view. Accepting others, no matter how different, is the challenge for developing a collegial approach to a community of learners. The following are examples of questions and comments that are typically shared between colleagues in a learning community:

- I hear what you are saying, but I still do not understand. Tell me more.
- You mentioned something yesterday that I have been thinking about. Would you be willing to talk more about it?
- I was not quite sure about the outcome of our meeting this afternoon. Can I check out my understanding with you because I may be way off?
- Before I jump to a conclusion about this, can I ask you about the note you left on my desk?

Encouraging individuals to take time for learning is a challenging task. The role of the educator is quite demanding, and time to learn new skills and new concepts often takes a backseat. The following suggested procedure describes a professional growth process that helps to encourage and validate adult learning and development.

Suggested Procedure: Encouraging Professional Growth

Many schools require teachers to participate in a professional growth process to encourage learning and skill development. As a part of this process, teachers may participate as members of peer study groups. These groups meet quarterly so that teachers can share their learning based on their individual professional growth goals. The purpose of having peer groups is to create a structure where teachers have opportunities to share what they have learned, where teachers can benefit from the learning of others, and where feedback and validation are provided in a safe, nonthreatening setting. The following is a sample format of a process where teachers go through a series of steps in developing and pursuing a long-range growth plan.

- Self-assessment
- Identification of the professional goal
- Identification of supporting objectives
- Participation in dialogue sessions with peer study groups to share individual plans
- Keeping a journal of impressions, insights, learning opportunities, and so on
- Presenting year-end results of benchmarks of success and results to peer study groups

HELPFUL HINT

Because any quality effort to pursue professional growth and improvement takes time, it is recommended that considerations be made for time available to teachers for such pursuits. Adjustments of expectations should reflect time built into the school calendar or schedule for professional development efforts. The more meaningful the process for pursuing professional growth, the more accepting and willing teachers will be to spend time focusing on their own learning.

One cannot underestimate the importance of the environment in organizational development. The school leader should work to provide opportunities for staff members to gain the skills necessary to effectively work with others. As staff members accept the premise that learning is ongoing, the quest for self-improvement and organizational improvement thrives. By accepting this change in view, we can begin to understand the need for new ways of thinking. The importance of these changes will be addressed in chapter 3.

Key Terms and Concepts

Active listening. The active listener takes equal responsibility in effective communication by appropriately responding, questioning, paraphrasing, and providing nonverbal cues that are genuine and respectful.

Communication stances. Virginia Satir has described four stances of communication typically taken by individuals under stress: placating, blaming, superreasonableness, and irrelevance.

Dialogue. In dialogue, individuals seek to go beyond their own understanding by taking in all points of view for the purpose of seeing the "big picture." The goal of dialogue is to have each person understand different perspectives on a situation versus individuals lobbying for a side or an opinion. The assumption is that the whole (big picture) is greater than the sum of its parts (individual points of view).

Discussion. To share points of view on a subject in order to formulate one single view.

Lifelong learner. The individual who strives to question, seeks new understanding, masters new skills, and strives to perfect old skills as a lifelong mission.

Organizational culture. Important environmental ingredients such as the values, beliefs, traditions, and attitudes that members of the organization have in common.

Sources

Bohm, D. (1985). *Unfolding meaning.* Mickleton, England: Foundation House.
Peck, S. (1987). *Different drum.* New York: Touchstone.
Satir, V. (1976). *Making contact.* Berkeley, CA: Celestial Arts.
Senge, P. (1990). *The fifth discipline: The art and practice of the learning organization.* New York: Doubleday.

Tulku, T. (1978). *Skillful means.* Berkeley, CA: Dharma Publishing.
Vaill, P. B. (1989). *Managing as a performing art.* San Francisco: Jossey-Bass.

Recommended Literature

Argyris, C. (1990). *Overcoming organizational defenses—Facilitating organizational learning.* Boston: Allyn & Bacon.
Avery, M., Auvina, B., Streibel, B., & Weiss, L. (Eds.). (1981). *Building united judgment.* Madison, WI: The Center for Conflict Resolution.
Byham, W. C. (1992). *Zapp! The lightning of empowerment.* New York: Ballantine.
Covey, S. R. (1989). *The 7 habits of highly effective people.* New York: Simon & Schuster.
Glasser, W. (1986). *Control theory in the classroom.* New York: Harper & Row.
Glenn, S. (1991a). *Developing capable young people.* Fair Oaks, CA: Developing Capable People Associates.
Glenn, S. (1991b). *Empowering others: Ten keys to affirming and validating people.* Fair Oaks, CA: Developing Capable People Associates.
Glenn, S. (1991c). *Involving and motivating people.* Fair Oaks, CA: Developing Capable People Associates.
Merenbloom, E. (1986). *The team process.* Columbus, OH: National Middle School Association.
Senge, P., & Lannon-Kim, C. (1991, November). Recapturing the spirit of learning through a systems approach. *The School Administrator,* pp. 8-13.

✧ 3 ✧

Exploring and Changing Mental Models

What Are Mental Models?

"Mental models are deeply ingrained assumptions, generalizations, or even pictures or images that influence how we understand the world and how we take action" (Senge, 1990). Quite often, we are not aware of the extent to which our behavior is affected by our mental models. Our attitudes and beliefs become a part of our thinking and are major factors in our perceptions of reality. It is through our mental models that we make sense of the world, determine right and wrong, evaluate ourselves and others, and decide what to do in the myriad of situations that face us on a daily basis.

Traditional school situations seem to be dominated by mental models that result in dependent or independent relationships. The dependent relationships evolve in hierarchical organizations where the administrators set the vision, make most of the decisions, and expect compliance. Some independent behaviors may arise in an organization where self-sufficiency and competition are encouraged. In these schools, the teacher role is viewed as time with students, and other staff members are viewed as supporters of teachers. Assumptions about people's lack of ability to deal with difficult situations often results in avoidance or political mediation. The general rule is that staff development programs necessitate the use of an "external expert." Parents, business, and others are viewed as visitors.

Schools that are managed by people whose mental models include a valuing of effective communication and collaboration tend to result in the development and maintenance of interdependent relationships.

- Decision making is inclusive and involves dialogue.
- Internal experts are developed and are expected to share their learning with others.
- A vision that is shared by all staff members is developed with facilitation by the administration.
- Difficult situations including conflict are addressed and are resolved through a process of communication and consensus building.
- Assumptions are consistently discussed, assessed, and adjusted to match the vision.
- All staff members take the responsibility for making good decisions and for following up with consistent actions.
- The role of all staff members is expanded to include planning, decision making, and other professional duties.
- Parents, business, and others are viewed as partners.
- The role of administrators is to empower people and inspire commitment.

Producing the results described in the vision, mission statement, or goals of any school is dependent on the alignment between the mental models of the staff and the desired results. Ideally, underlying values, beliefs, and assumptions would be discussed prior to and during the process of visioning or goal setting. If the words used to define the vision are not consistent with the paradigms governing the actions of the staff, the vision will be meaningless. Bringing mental models to the surface, examining them, and determining the necessity for potential changes is an essential but time-consuming process. Most often, schools are satisfied to work with the commitment of a few and the compliance of most in the hope that progress will occur. Time spent working with, rather than ignoring, mental models can mean an increase in the potential of progress occurring and being maintained over time.

Examining Existing Mental Models

Although mental models are deeply ingrained and extremely powerful, change is possible. The first step is awareness. School staff members must have opportunities to examine their beliefs and assumptions on both an individual and a group basis. Because mental models are deeply rooted in values and assumptions, the process of examination and assessment should be carefully planned and executed. Before any improvement can be made, an awareness of existing mental models and of their power over behavior must be established.

Existing paradigms or mental models for people working in schools come from both personal information and experience and from current and historical, widely held beliefs about education. These paradigms should be surfaced and examined. When possible, they should be analyzed for degree of alignment with the goals of the organization. One challenge in dealing with mental models is that they tend to be an unconscious part of people's thinking and behavior. Bringing the mental models into consciousness is difficult.

A safe place to begin examining mental models is with the beliefs about education. Use of a topic that is somewhat removed from the personal beliefs of individual staff members can begin to establish the habit of delving into the underlying assumptions that produce decisions, policies, and behaviors that affect everyone in schools, including students. Practicing this habit can also help individuals to become more aware of their own beliefs.

Possible topics include the following:

- The school year should begin in September and end in May.
- Problem-solving skills are an important aspect of math instruction.
- Standardized test scores are valid indicators of a school's effectiveness.
- Having students work in groups produces cooperative behaviors.
- The success of the United States in the world market tomorrow is dependent on the methodologies used in classes today.

- All students can learn.
- Class size plays an important role in student-teacher interaction.
- School administrators should be instructional leaders.
- The rate of students dropping out of schools is greater now than it was in the earlier part of this century.
- The amount of homework assigned is an indicator of student learning.

Examination of mental models will only take place if the practice of doing so is scheduled regularly thus indicating a valuing of time spent in this effort. The following suggested procedure will assist the school leader in helping staff members examine mental models.

Suggested Procedure 1: Examining Mental Models

Step 1: During a scheduled staff meeting or in-service, set aside time for discussion of one of the topics listed above. Prior to the meeting, inform staff members about the topic and ask that they begin thinking about the beliefs, assumptions, and values that might lead to the statement that will be discussed.

Step 2: Depending on the size of the whole group, small discussion groups may be assigned. In the assignment of staff members to groups, consideration should be given to the desirability of either job-alike or job-different groupings.

Step 3: Assign the topic and the following discussion questions to each group:
 a. What assumptions are inherent in this viewpoint?
 b. What perceptions of time, right or wrong, good or bad, value, cause or effect, and so on are insinuated?
 c. Are there any generalizations involved in this viewpoint?
 d. What theories might lead to this viewpoint?
 e. What images might be produced by this viewpoint?

f. What actions might be influenced by this viewpoint?
Step 4: Share conclusions, reports from each group.
Step 5: Ask individuals the following questions: (a) What new insights were gained? and (b) How might this activity be used for self-reflection?

Examining personal mental models requires honest reflection and self-assessment. This step of the process is more difficult. The skills and habits of reflection and self-assessment must be taught. Individuals who are involved in activities that require exposing core values or beliefs are often surprised to realize how little experience they have had with such a self-examination. Although schools and school districts are regularly engaged in the writing of mission statements, goals, and objectives, many staff members have not been involved in an assessment of their personal mental models. In addition, they have not had many opportunities to learn that their images of how the world works may differ from the images maintained by others. We often judge other people based on differing behaviors or opinions, but do not take the time to understand the basis for the differences.

The purpose of examining personal mental models is not to determine who is right and who is wrong. There is no appropriate, accurate, or best paradigm for how the world works or for what is most important. Individuals and groups must do their best to first understand their own mental models and those of others and then to build shared mental models that are most likely to produce the results desired.

Style delineators are tools that are helpful for increasing the awareness of personal mental models. The following suggested procedure shares insights about the use of these tools.

Suggested Procedure 2: Awareness of Personal Mental Models

Style delineators are useful tools for self-examination. A number of tools such as 4-MAT, True Colors, Gregorc, and Meyers-Briggs are available for use in staff in-service. Through the questionnaires and activities that are included in most activities of this type, an individual can gain a greater understanding of personal

38 ❖ Structuring Schools for Success

values and paradigms. Most style delineators include information about stretching oneself into the use of other paradigms, of not valuing one style over another, and of the importance of attempting to understand all types of viewpoints.

As powerful as individual mental models are, group mental models have even more influence over behavior. Support for behaviors that are based on commonly held beliefs and values encourages the continuation and frequency of those behaviors. The results produced by group mental models can be positive or negative. Benefits depend partially on the congruence between the group mental models and the desired outcomes of the school. Because groups of students are very much affected by the mental models that prevail in the classroom and in the school, the combined results of the group choices and behaviors should be examined. Depending on the organizational structure of the school, this may involve grade-level teams, departments, special groups such as committees, support staff, and so on.

Once individuals have had an opportunity to examine their own personal mental models, it is beneficial to use this information in the analysis of group characteristics and dynamics. The following procedure is helpful in using the information learned from style delineators in developing a group perspective.

Suggested Procedure 3: Group Mental Models

> Step 1: Assign staff members to job-alike groups. Ideally, choose groupings of staff members that work together with a particular group of students or adults.
>
> Step 2: Depending on the style delineator that has been used previously with individuals, provide each group with a grid for the purpose of charting the predominant styles of each group member.
>
> Step 3: Assign each group to complete the grid. Ask them to study the dominant styles of their group.
>
> Step 4: Assign each group to answer the following questions:
> a. Does the group have a dominant style or does there appear to be a balance?

Exploring and Changing Mental Models ❖ 39

   b. What are the general implications of the image represented by this grid?
   c. What will the group need to consider in order to work together most effectively?
   d. What might the team need to do in order to achieve a balanced effect when meeting, discussing issues, and attempting to reach consensus?
   e. What are the implications for the strategies that are likely to be prevalent as the group works with students, parents, or other teams?
Step 5: Group reports. Assign each group to report the conclusions that they have derived from their discussion.
Step 6: Ask each group the following questions:
   a. What insights were gained?
   b. How might this activity be used for further team improvement?

HELPFUL HINT

Another stage in the process of examining mental models is to develop an awareness of the differences between beliefs and assumptions held by various staff members. At some point in the process, alignment with desired results or vision will become apparent and will be necessary. Initially, the purpose of activities is to increase the awareness that differences exist and to motivate inquiry about mental models held by others.

As groups learn about the different mental models that exist in an organization, it is important to teach individuals how to recognize these differences and how to deal with them. The following suggested procedure will assist the school leader by offering a process focused in a school setting.

Suggested Procedure 4: Awareness of Differing Mental Models

Using the concept of the "fish bowl" or "kiva," participants are asked to respond to the same question while others listen.

Step 1: Assign participants to job-alike groups. Examples: teachers from each grade level, office staff, special education teachers, parents, students, support staff, and so on.

Step 2: Ask participants to spend a few moments reflecting on their answer to a predetermined question.
   a. How would you describe the evaluation process in this school? (procedures, policies, time lines, key players, history, attitudes, possibility of changes, etc.)
   b. How would you describe the discipline process in this school? (same suggested aspects as above)
   c. How would you describe the budgeting process in this school? (same suggested aspects as above)

Step 3: Have each group take a turn in the center circle. Time should be allowed for each individual to respond and for some dialogue to take place. Other participants should be seated in a larger outer circle. They should be instructed to listen only but to pay attention to the mental models that underlie the descriptions of how the system operates. Allow each group to have a turn in the center circle.

Step 4: Ask each group the following questions:
   a. What mental models appeared to be most prevalent?
   b. What mental models appear to represent differing assumptions?
   c. How might these differing assumptions have been formed?

Next steps: Depending on the comfort level of the group, it may be necessary to stop at this point and to continue at another time. At some point, it is necessary to identify the mental models that best match the desired results of each process within the school organization. When working with existing processes, it is best to achieve consensus about shared mental models and to adapt the processes if necessary. When designing new processes, the practice of identifying related assumptions, beliefs, generalizations, and/or images can be built into the design procedures.

RISK FACTORS

The mental models adopted by each individual were formed by the life experiences of that individual. Exposing personal mental models can be threatening, especially if certain paradigms are not "popular." Individuals may have little or no experience with examining their own assumptions and may be worried about the potential results. Anger or denial may result.

HELPFUL HINT

It is important to make any exercise involving mental models as safe and nonthreatening as possible. Participants should be assured that all mental models are valid and valuable. Progress toward identifying desirable mental models should be accompanied by encouragement and support for changes in thinking and behavior.

Adopting New Mental Models as Necessary

As awareness and understanding of mental models is increased, it is likely that some mental models will appear to be better aligned with the goals and efforts of the organization than others. Adopting new mental models does not happen by choosing whose mental models are right and whose are wrong. It is through a well-defined culture (described in chapter 2) that norms for behavior are established. Through information, training, and experience, individuals learn that certain mental models facilitate the occurrence of those behaviors and others inhibit it.

Continual opportunities to clarify beliefs, to test assumptions, and to acquire knowledge and experience assist staff members in making decisions about the fit between their mental models and the goals and efforts of the organization. As a result of these opportunities, staff members are better able to set career goals. Possible career goals include adapting one's mental models and finding an organization where one's existing mental models are a better fit. The process of having individuals clarify personal visions and having groups build and clarify a shared vision (discussed in chapter 4) is a natural step after examining and testing mental models.

There are few tools or strategies available for testing assumptions that help to determine when it is appropriate and/or important to adopt new mental models. The following suggested procedure describes some technological tools available that can assist in this process.

Suggested Procedure: Testing Assumptions

Although dialogue and discussion can be useful in surfacing assumptions, few processes exist for actually testing the assumed connections between beliefs and actions. Life's experiences can prove to be risky testing grounds for our mental models. Training and computer software (STELLA) available through High Performance Systems, Inc. can provide individuals with useful tools. Through the process of creating a computer simulation, the effects of certain assumptions on the behavior of a system can be modeled. Computer technology allows us to go beyond the power of our observations in "real time" and into the observation of changes in systems in "simulated time." Training in system dynamics and in the associated field of systems thinking is recommended as a strategy for increasing the ability to surface and to test mental models. Such training can help people to realize the power of mental models and to realize the importance of aligning mental models with desired results.

Only by adapting mental models can change be implemented. The process of building a shared vision (described in chapter 4) is dependent on individual readiness to describe a personal vision but also to perhaps "let go" of a part of that personal vision for the sake of a vision valued by the majority. The goal of adopting new mental models is not to get everyone to think alike. Water Lippman, an American journalist, once said, "Where all think alike, no one thinks very much." The organization being described in this book should be full of individuals who think a great deal. Part of that thinking should be constantly assessing the usefulness of mental models and adapting them as necessary.

The process of adapting mental models should be accompanied by information, resource materials, dialogue, and support. All of these are necessary because of the challenges inherent in the process of change. As the process is evolving, it is important for the building administrator to remember the following:

- Changing mental models takes time but is essential to changing behavior. (Teachers who do not believe that all students can learn will have trouble implementing the mainstreaming of special education students.)
- In the beginning, staff members may respond with anxiety and uncertainty. (The challenge to long-held beliefs can create insecurity about an individual's decision making and performance.)
- As the change is taking place, practice is essential. (Giving minilessons about topics such as locus of control, dialogue, and interdependence, and then assigning individual or group tasks of a developmentally appropriate nature can create new habits and confidence.)
- As the change is taking place, feedback is essential. (Monitoring progress and recognizing milestones—such as consistent modeling of a new assumption or understanding that is verbalized, and celebrating them in a dignifying manner—can encourage further growth.)
- Using mentoring by peers can be effective. (In some situations, purposeful matching of colleagues into peer-coaching situations for the purpose of adapting mental models in addition to more traditional coaching about instructional strategies can create a sense of partnership and security.)
- A belief in the human ability to adapt to change is crucial. (In the history of education, many changes have been demanded but many have also been assumed to be impossible. A belief that the vast majority of educators want what is best for students and that they will adapt beliefs and habits if they see potential benefits for students provides motivation for leaders to tackle situations that appear difficult to change.)

The pressure for educational change is great. There are many demands for the production of new and better results. Although change is difficult, we can learn from past attempts, both successful and unsuccessful. In education as in other fields, understanding and support of the desired results is a key to success. Building that understanding and support can be facilitated by an awareness of the power of mental models and the importance of aligning mental models with desired results.

Key Terms and Concepts

Alignment. Match or consistency between various parts of a system.

Dependent relationships. Relationships that result in an inability to operate in isolation. Actions taken in one area cannot occur without causal actions in other areas.

Desired results. Goals, objectives, mission statements, vision statements, and other descriptions of outcomes that are desirable.

Fish bowl or kiva. An activity in which one group of participants engages in dialogue in the center of a circle while other participants listen.

Independent relationships. Relationships that result in an ability to operate in isolation. Actions taken in one area have no effect on other areas.

Mental models. Assumptions, beliefs, attitudes, perceptions of reality.

STELLA. A computer software program that allows the user to design a model and simulate the dynamic behavior of a system over time.

Style delineators. Tools such as the Meyers-Briggs, the Gregorc, 4-MAT, or True Colors that help individuals to classify their preferences and behaviors into categories.

Source

Senge, P. (1990). *The fifth discipline: The art and practice of the learning organization.* New York: Doubleday

Recommended Literature

Covey, S. R. (1989). *The 7 habits of highly effective people.* New York: Simon & Schuster.

Covey, S. R. (1991). *Principle-centered leadership.* New York: Simon & Schuster.

DePree, M. (1989). *Leadership is an art.* New York: Doubleday.

Gregorc, A. (1982). *An adult's guide to style.* Maynard, MA: Gabriel Systems.

Hammer, A. L. (1987). *An introduction to type (Meyers-Briggs).* Palo Alto, CA: Consulting Psychologists Press.

Hickman, C. R. (1992). *Mind of a manager, soul of a leader.* New York: John Wiley.

McCarthy, B. (1987). *The 4 MAT system.* Barrington, IL: EXCEL.

Pressel, L., & Gardner, R. H. (1992). *Supervision for empowered workers—New leadership styles for self-managing teams.* Bisbee, AZ: Loma Linda.

Roberts, N., Andersen, D., Deal, R., Garet, M., & Shaffer, W. (1983). *Introduction to computer simulation: A system dynamics modeling approach.* Reading, MA: Addison-Wesley.

Smith, W. F., & Andrews, R. L. (1989). *Instructional leadership—How principals make a difference.* Alexandria, VA: Association for Supervision and Curriculum Development.

STELLA II modeling software. (1990). Hanover, NH: High Performance Systems.

True colors. (1988). Laguna Beach, CA: Communication Companies International.

✦ 4 ✦

Determining the Desired Results of the Organization

Defining Desired Results

How often do people in an organization ask the question, "What exactly are we trying to accomplish?"

Organizations often get so caught up in everyday operations that the actual desired results of the organization become lost. The desired results of an educational organization are the outcomes, conditions, skills, and abilities that are ultimately the goal and essence of the system. If these desired results are achieved, then the organization is seen as successful and productive.

In education, the opinions of many stakeholders help to determine desired results. Educators, parents, students, community members, and district, state, and federal officials are stakeholders who have strong beliefs about the results that educational systems should produce.

- Are these results always congruent?
- What happens when members from different stakeholder groups disagree?
- What happens when members of the same stakeholder group disagree?
- Do parents all agree about what students should achieve?
- Do educators agree about what outcomes students should produce?

Seldom do people have the same viewpoint when assessing the same social system about what is right, necessary, and important. Almost everyone has had experience in educational systems. The experiences of parents, businesspeople, government officials, and community members are varied from different geographical locations, from the private and public sectors, and from different points in time, resulting in a variety of mental models about what education should look like or be.

When stakeholders disagree about the results they think schools should produce, the ambiguity increases in deciding what we need to do to improve our educational system. It is by bringing all of these varying mental models together that we can begin to derive a common set of desired results for today's educational system. When education fails to address the importance of bringing together the mental models of all stakeholders, the system responds to immediate needs without examining the long-term consequences of decisions. Thus, much like trying to shoot an arrow at a moving target, it is difficult to focus and align structures within the school to best achieve outcomes resulting in success. In chapter 5, the importance of aligning structures with desired results will be described and illustrated.

Before an organization attempts to determine desired results, it is important to clarify the personal visions of each member of the organization. These personal visions can be used to build a shared vision of the organization. The shared vision can then be broken down to specific desired results of the school organization. A vision is an abstract view or picture. Desired results are the results that would be produced if the vision was real.

In this chapter, a process moving from personal vision to shared vision to desired results will be explained and illustrated.

Clarifying Personal Vision

Where does one start? The first step is the clarification of personal visions by examining individual beliefs and mental models, and asking the following questions of ourselves and our staff members.

- What do we want the organization to accomplish? For students? For staff? For community?
- What will the results look like? From the point of view of students? From the point of view of staff? From the point of view of community?
- How different is my view of success from others? From students? From those I work with? From community?

Chapter 3 discussed the importance of providing opportunities for examining mental models, personal beliefs, and assumptions. By honestly reflecting on the questions above, individuals will begin to clarify their own vision of their school setting. This is a crucial step in moving toward the creation of a shared vision with clearly articulated desired results in a school organization. This sample activity will provide a process for clarifying personal vision.

Suggested Procedure: Personal-Vision Exercise

Provide each staff member several index cards and ask each of them to write down words, phrases, images, or diagrams of what they see as their vision of the school. Provide a quiet, reflective atmosphere for this initial task. Depending on how many opportunities staff members have had to reflect on their personal vision of the school, this activity may appear frustrating for some and quite easy for others (15 minutes).

RISK FACTORS

By emphasizing that only words and phrases are desired, the comfort level of the group should increase. There is no need for long narratives and sophisticated prose on the index cards. This activity may be modified by asking staff members to answer specific questions rather than allowing for the openness of describing their personal vision. The above-mentioned questions would help serve this purpose. The degree of specificity of the task should be carefully planned and designed by considering the participating individuals.

Evolution of a Shared Vision

A shared vision is much more than a statement of mission or a collection of descriptors. It is a governing force guiding each member of the organization, as measured by the consistency of the beliefs, values, and assumptions with the everyday decisions and behaviors of the members. A shared vision is not stagnant but dynamic, as the organization develops and evolves.

Vision is simply not just one person's view articulated to another, but a shared set of common images that provides us with the answer to the question, "What do we really want to create?" It is only from the personal visions of organizational members that shared visions do truly evolve. A shared vision cannot be created and sustained without a carefully planned process for its development (Senge, 1990, pp. 205-232).

Each and every member of the organization should be able to demonstrate his or her commitment to the vision through the decisions he or she makes about his or her own behaviors. The guiding strength of a shared vision lies in each and every member's ability to behave consistently and contribute positively to the realization of the vision.

What can a shared vision do? It can create a sense of commonality that strengthens the organization and that brings coherence and common purpose in the face of diversity. By forming connections and bonding people together by a common aspiration, a shared vision can foster risk taking and experimentation. Each individual can then see the organization as a whole, sharing responsibility for the whole and not just the part in which he or she is involved.

As the shared vision is developed, it can provide a regenerating energy and focus to the organization that is invigorating and motivational. A shared vision can serve as the lighthouse in times of chaos and upheaval, by providing light and guidance, helping members manage more confidently the dynamics of troubling situations.

The following suggested procedure describes how a shared vision can evolve after personal visions have been clarified. This process is appropriate in any school setting and should involve all staff members.

50 ✧ Structuring Schools for Success

Suggested Procedure: The Evolution of a Shared Vision

Step 1: Do personal-vision exercise described above.

Step 2: In groups that represent varying roles within the school (6 to 8 people each), ask individuals to share in their small group the descriptors on their index cards. Each group should designate a recorder. Without agreeing or disagreeing with shared words, phrases, or images, the group should find the common words or common threads shared by all individuals in the group. Choose only those things that were clearly agreed on unanimously. There may be only a few, but discussion should not lead to certain opinions winning out.

Step 3: The group should then plan a presentation that represents and clearly communicates the common aspects of their personal vision to the entire staff or larger group. Choices for presentations may include skit, role-play, poetry, song, dialogue, art, and so on. The presentation should be brief (approximately 5 minutes each) but should depict clearly the common visionary threads of the small group.

Step 4: Small groups present their visions to the large group. A recorder should write down on chart paper all of the words, phrases, and/or images that they hear or see in each presentation.

Step 5: During a break, the facilitators or small-group representatives should condense the large group's list recorded during the presentations by condensing repeated words or phrases, thoughts, images, or ideas. The result should be a list of words, phrases, diagrams, or images that were shared with the large group.

RISK FACTORS

Any time individuals are asked to present their thoughts or ideas to a large group, it can be risky. Oftentimes, small groups choose to use humor to help make the presentation safer. This is not to be discouraged. This activity can be very enjoyable for the group because groups oftentimes tap their creative spirits and sense of humor when planning and presenting the small-group common visions to the larger group. Even though visioning activities are serious, important business, a sense of fun is crucial for participating individuals.

Clarifying Shared Vision

As the members of an organization begin to realize the vision they share, it is essential to work to clarify the vision beyond mere words or exercises. A shared vision is only useful if it guides the actions of individuals in the organization. A list of words or phrases or concise statements of mission are not useful unless practiced and continually clarified.

As described in chapter 2, dialogue is a useful tool in helping an organization to clarify a shared vision. By selecting an aspect of the vision and having open dialogue about individual perceptions, assumptions, examples, and beliefs, one can begin to seek the true meaning of that aspect. For example, if one aspect of an organization's shared vision is the value of asking questions, the meaning for that vague and broad aspect may mean many different things to different people. For example, during a dialogue differing opinions may include (a) a belief that questioning is the essence of learning; (b) a belief that by asking questions, a slow-down in the learning process results; or (c) a belief that there is an appropriate time and place for questions. By examining different points of view, one can then flush out the specifics of the vision by truly seeing "what it may look like."

Because the shared vision is forever evolving, it is important to recognize that as new members join the organization, they should each be actively invited to contribute to clarifying the existing vision. Knowing that the vision is not stagnant, the addition of new perspectives and ideas should be valued and pursued. The vision thus spreads and evolves in a dynamic, changing process.

The comfort level of the organization, as it embraces new perspectives and ideas, can be viewed as a process of "organizational maturity." Organizational maturity is the ability of individuals in the organization to (a) consistently articulate and describe the shared vision through words and actions, (b) see challenges facing the organization as learning opportunities, (c) accept the fact that the only perfection is imperfection, and (d) willingly consider the ideas and beliefs of others for they provide important views that cannot be seen from within. Conditions in a system are always changing. When the members of an organization recognize that they have the power to control the conditions, they become empowered. Thus striving for improvement by developing the belief that all organizational members are learners brings about growth and maturity in the organization. As organizations work toward developing a shared vision, they will mature into learning organizations, striving for improvement, for the purpose of educational quality.

Understanding the evolving nature of the shared vision requires constant clarification of what the vision really looks like in the school setting. The vision is clarified when individuals move from using mere words to describe the vision to connecting the observable, daily behaviors and actions of individuals in the organization to the vision. The following suggested procedure describes several possibilities for clarifying the shared vision.

Suggested Procedure: Clarifying the Shared Vision

- Shared-vision lunches: Periodically schedule potluck luncheons where a specific aspect of the shared vision may be the focus of staff dialogue. As people first come together and eat, provide wall space for individuals to write comments, draw pictures, or share quotes or cartoons that help describe the daily topic. (Topics could come from the shared-vision exercise described earlier.) The comments on the walls can help stimulate a dialogue that will bring further meaning to the words that describe the aspect of the vision.
- Share an interaction or situation in which you felt or behaved consistently with the shared vision of the school. Share the situation at a meeting, through a written note, computer E-mail, or a brief conversation. Communicate to all staff members that this sharing is valued and helps the evolution of the vision.
- Seek out feedback from visitors or outsiders who have experienced your school in some way. Openly, share and

celebrate the consistencies of the shared vision they communicate through their feedback.
- Role-play exercise: Ask the staff members to describe the shared vision of the school, using any mode of communication they see fit, to an alien school superintendent visiting the planet earth. Having a true outsider (principal from another school, district office administrator, university professor, etc.) acting the role of the alien can be helpful as you ask him or her as a visitor to articulate his or her understanding of the shared vision at the end of the exercise. This provides the staff members with feedback about how clearly they communicate the evolving vision of their organization in a fun and nonthreatening way. It can also help educate others who may want to learn more about the school they are visiting. This activity can be done in small groups making brief presentations to the fictional superintendent.

Deriving Desired Results From a Shared Vision

The shared vision provides the organization with a general area of focus, and desired results can be seen as the specific steps for achieving outcomes desired within the organizational vision. When organizations have invested time clarifying and defining the parameters of the shared vision, the desired results become necessary in accurately assessing the productivity of the organizations. Therefore, the movement is from a clear focus that evolves through the visioning process to the specificity of deriving desired results.

Much like the master teacher who moves from a general curricular focus to the specificity of a succinct, well-planned lesson, the carefully planned establishment of desired results is essential to the success and development of the organization. The master teacher defines specific learning outcomes and a variety of strategies to meet the varying needs of students. The leader of the organization must make plans, moving step-by-step, based on the readiness, abilities, and past experiences of the staff members. Like students, it is important to consider staff members as having differing mental models (as discussed in chapter 2), different learning styles, and varying degrees of willingness to accept change. These factors will directly affect how desired results are derived.

Taking into consideration the diversity among the typical school staff, well-established working groups within the school are the best vehicle for deriving desired results from the shared vision. Keeping the vision fresh and alive for individuals is a key factor in creating desired results that will be consistent with the vision. In a group setting, seeking common viewpoints of desired results of the school requires group skills, including effective communication and collaboration as discussed in chapter 2. A team or group of individuals can clarify the shared vision together, then examine the various viewpoints within the group, specifying the desired results that are clear, understood by all, and can be assessed as results through formal and informal measures.

Before an organization works to determine desired results, the importance of revisiting the shared vision of the organization should not be underestimated. Because a vision evolves as changes in conditions and personnel occur, it is essential to continue to revisit the vision as the organization assesses and plans for the future. The following suggested procedure describes one possible process.

Suggested Procedure 1: Revisiting the Vision

> Step 1: Using a Kiva or fish bowl format (see chapter 3), have small groups of individuals (better to mix individuals with different organizational roles) role-play the various stakeholders in your school community. In a timed segment, have them dialogue about what they believe the current vision or direction of the school is as determined by current practices. Stakeholder groups may include students, staff members, and parents. To enable them to role-play stakeholder groups that are different than the ones they belong to, provide surveys, letters, feedback, editorials, meeting minutes, or any other information that supplies accurate information about viewpoints of current practices. Ask those on the outside of the circle to listen to the various viewpoints they hear from different stakeholder groups.

Determining Desired Results ✧ 55

Step 2: In job-alike groups (grade-level teams, department groups, classified personnel, etc.), have individuals share what common themes and inconsistencies they may have heard. This is a time for dialogue about what individuals heard during the Kiva exercise.

Once the vision is clarified, individuals must move from the abstract picture of the shared vision to the specific results the organization desires to produce. Rather than facilitating this process with the entire staff, it is suggested to begin the process in job-alike groups. The following suggested procedure has helped groups involved in curriculum revision, goal setting, and strategic planning.

Suggested Procedure 2: Deriving Desired Results

Step 1: Have groups make decisions about team or group results that they would like to achieve. A suggested process for this task would be to have individuals in teams or work groups brainstorm a list of possible results that the team or work group could achieve during the upcoming school year. Brainstorming rules would not allow discussion or judgments of individual ideas. All ideas should be accepted and compiled in a group list. This activity can be done in grade-level teams, department groups, or job-alike groups. This is also an effective activity for student groups such as student committees, student council, community service groups, and so on.

Step 2: Inform individuals that they will be voting for the results that they feel are most important for their group and for the school. Ask if any clarifications are needed for any of the ideas on the brainstorm list. Remind all individuals that they should have a clear understanding of what each idea for desired results represents.

Step 3: The group will then prioritize the list of results through a voting process. Each individual is given three differently colored dots that will have varying weight assigned to them. For example, blue dots may be worth three votes, red dots two votes, and yellow dots one vote.

Individuals should place their blue dot next to the result that they feel is the most important, the red for the next important result, and so on. After all members have finished their priority voting, a facilitator can compute the votes and derive the group priorities. It is important to note then that the color of the dot will influence the importance of the result, not just the number of dots placed next to an item.

Step 4: When groups see the priorities that they have established, the facilitator should ask them to support the group decision even if the top results are not the same as individual choices. This is an important part of the process where individuals may need to let go of strong personal opinions and feelings. Visible signs of frustration should be addressed before moving to the next steps. A verbal vote of support and/or commitment to the group's decision should precede moving to steps in making future plans.

HELPFUL HINTS

This activity works well at the end of the year when assessing the organization and making plans for the upcoming school year. After teams or work groups derive desired results for the forthcoming year, they may use the summer to focus on the group-desired results through reflection and possible summer team planning. The staff members can then return to school after the summer break with a clear focus of what they want to accomplish. Specific desired results are also very helpful for students and parents as they learn about the expectations of the approaching school year. Open houses and orientations are good opportunities to present and explain the desired results for the upcoming school year.

The process of deriving desired results from a shared vision is not only exciting but provides a clear direction for the development of the organization. The next step, described in chapter 5, involves the identification and the alignment of the structures of an organization that increase the likelihood that the desired results will be achieved.

Key Terms and Concepts

Desired results. The desired results are the outcomes, conditions, skills, and abilities that are the specific goals of the organization that are derived from the shared vision.

Organizational maturity. The comfort level of the organization, as it embraces new perspectives and ideas and as it plans for changing conditions within the organizational system.

Personal vision. The beliefs, assumptions, and mental model of an individual.

Shared vision. A governing force guiding each member of the organization, as measured by the consistency of the beliefs, values, and assumptions with the everyday decisions and behaviors of the members.

Stakeholders. Individuals who are directly or indirectly affected by the practices and outcomes of the organization. In education, stakeholder groups may include students, staff, parents, community members, business groups, and so on.

Source

Senge, P. (1990). *The fifth discipline: The art and practice of the learning organization.* New York: Doubleday.

Recommended Literature

Edelman, M. W. (1992). *The measure of our success.* Boston: Beacon.
Fritz, R. (1989). *The path of least resistance.* New York: Ballantine.
Fritz, R. (1991). *Creating.* New York: Ballantine.
Parker, M. (1990). *Creating shared vision.* Clarendon Hills, IL: Dialog International.
Perry, N. J. (1990, January). Computers come of age in class. *Fortune Magazine,* pp. 72-78.

✧ 5 ✧

Adjusting Organizational Structures

Aligning Organizational Structures With Desired Results

Following the identification of desired results as described in chapter 4, structures within the organization should be examined and aligned. Structures in a system include the following:

- Organizational design: job descriptions, ongoing work teams, and other groups that are convened as necessary, hierarchy, lack of hierarchy, and so on
- Policies: written and unwritten rules and guidelines for procedures and practices
- Practices: behaviors, actions, strategies, activities, and so on that are used by both individuals and groups
- Mental models: attitudes, beliefs, values, assumptions, and generalizations that affect decisions we make and behaviors that we choose

The match or alignment between structures of a system and the results that the system is attempting to produce is a major determinant of success.

Current trends in school organization tend toward shared involvement in and responsibility for decision making. Site-based management is based on committees formed around the needs and goals of the school. Designs that include the concepts related to Total Quality Management (TQM) require collaboration to adhere to the 14 principles that are intended to guide actions. Other types of participatory management also require that educators work together in ways that are new to them and that are challenging even with commitment and practice. These organizational components can only be successful if they are well aligned with desired results. However, the structures alone will not improve education.

The policies and practices of a school can be both obvious and subtle. As desired results are clarified and organizational structures are aligned, it is necessary to have policies and practices that also support and facilitate the production of desired results. Some indication of alignment can be gained through a study of written policies and practices. This can be done with task groups assigned to analyze particular sets of policies, rules, or guidelines.

Further examination is necessary to attain a full picture. Individual and group behaviors are often governed by unwritten policies and traditional practices. A match between desired results and policies will not be sufficient unless behaviors are also consistent.

Consistency between behavior and desired results is an essential element of organizational maturity. The hectic pace of normal school routines often leaves little time for identification of behaviors that best fit the vision. The result is often a wide spectrum of behaviors, some of which are unproductive and/or inhibiting. Guiding staff members through activities that require reflection and dialogue about aligning behaviors is very much like coaching a teacher to choose instructional strategies that most likely match lesson objectives. The following suggested procedure should be helpful as the leader coaches and guides.

Suggested Procedure: Aligning Behaviors

Step 1: Choose a set of desired results and a group of people that are responsible for producing those results.

Step 2: Assign the group to study each desired result and to describe behaviors that are likely to be supportive.
  a. What actions might a person take to produce this result?
  b. What considerations might be evident in decision making?
  c. What types of activities might be planned for students or others involved?

d. What types of interaction might be evident?

Step 3: Engage the group in a discussion about the behaviors that are listed.
   a. Is there agreement about all behaviors?
   b. Do the lists of behaviors seem to be complete?
   c. Could a person who is new to the school use the list as a basis for decision making and behavior?
   d. If there are disagreements about some areas, what are the reasons for the differences of perception?

Step 4: Lists of agreed on behaviors can be used as guidelines for the group but should be reexamined on a regular basis.

Step 5: Behaviors for which there is not a consensus should be examined. It is most likely that the disagreements result from differences in mental models.

RISK FACTOR

As mentioned in previous chapters, asking staff members to examine their own behaviors can be threatening. Activities such as the one described above can only be done in an atmosphere of trust and personal responsibility. Staff members must see themselves as influential factors in the overall results that the school produces. They must have had opportunities to see connections between their classrooms and other aspects of the school. The procedure suggested should be used after a high level of organizational maturity has been achieved.

As discussed in chapter 3, all people possess mental models—beliefs, assumptions, and generalizations—that greatly influence their actions. Changing behaviors requires the changing of mental models. In many cases, an analysis of the results that are produced by different behaviors can lead to personal reflection and a personal decision to make changes. If additional changes are necessary, staff members should have opportunities to engage in dialogue, training, and other activities that will allow them to expand their mental models and that will give them opportunities to adapt. Mismatched mental models and behaviors that persist must usually be dealt with on an individual basis. This administrative task is part of the coaching and the evaluation that are required in all schools. Strategies such as those involved in cognitive coaching (Costa, 1989) are helpful tools.

The greater the alignment between the structures—organization, policies, practices, and mental models—and the desired results of a school or school district, the greater the potential for producing desired results. The structures can contribute to or detract from the capacity to achieve the outcomes that are envisioned. For example, we cannot expect successful implementation of integrated curriculum without implementing the structure of interdisciplinary teams. Interdisciplinary teams cannot be effective unless the individuals involved possess the skills necessary to work together.

The Concept of Leverage

The concept of leverage is based on appropriate use of simple tools to manage difficult situations. Just as we can use levers to move large objects, we can use the concept of leverage to make adjustments in complex organizations. Developing schools today to meet the needs of tomorrow is certainly complex. It is especially challenging because of the incredible rate of change that is evident in our society. In the midst of the need to reform, it is advantageous to consider possible sources of assistance to help us understand and use leverage.

One source of assistance in determining points of leverage is a field of study called system dynamics.

> System dynamics is the most fully developed technology for modeling complex dynamic systems, and especially those where cause and effect are neither closely related in space nor time. As a person looks for places where there is leverage for making changes to obtain improvement, he/she is inevitably brought into the realm of synthesis. The changes often amount to . . . changing the structure, the very crux of synthesis. (Brown, 1990)

The tools of system dynamics include creating computer simulations that model the behavior of a system being studied. Work is currently under way by many experts to design computer simulations that are related to the field of education. Up until this point, most efforts have been concentrated on other world situations. A new focus on the important relationship between system dynamics and school organizations is becoming a tremendous resource for many schools across the country. While the application of this field of study is evolving, we can adapt some of the basic concepts such as leverage to increase the potential of bringing about more effective change in education.

An understanding of how schools work is a necessary step to the improvement of education and must involve thinking in a more systemic way. This expanded mode of thinking requires seeing schools as systems made up of many interdependent relationships. Increased understanding of these relationships can lead to identification of leverage actions. These actions will often involve small, subtle changes that produce large results because of their effect on many aspects of the organization. Looking for small changes that make big differences requires a move away from more common problem-solving strategies that tend to cause the choosing of grand action plans. These action plans are often put into place, steps are implemented as planned, and no assessment of results is conducted until the final step is completed. A historical perspective on education would show that many grand plans resulted in tremendous resistance and ultimate failure. Even without resistance, the first step of an action plan can produce very different results than predicted. A new process of decision making can help educators to avoid undesired long-term results. The first steps of an action plan are initiated, then the results produced by those steps are assessed, followed by an appropriate adjustment of next steps. Small, initial steps are much more likely to perform as levers for future actions if decision makers exercise patience and conduct an analysis of current conditions and relationships, and a synthesis of all that is known can result.

The Concept of Feedback

Often an overused term, *feedback* is the vehicle that provides us with information about the results that our behavior and decisions are producing. Purposeful management is the careful decision-making process used when making additions, deletions, and modifications in organizational structures while using feedback generated from the stakeholders of the organization. The process includes the following:

- Collection of feedback based on desired results
- Synthesis of feedback
- Examination of current structures and practices
- Making decisions about adjustments in structures or practices
- Implementation of the adjustments and "running the changes"
- Collection of more feedback, and so on

Collecting feedback can be done formally or informally as matched with the needs and style of the organization. District surveys, standardized tests, school opinion polls, and parent questionnaires are all examples of formal methodologies. Formal methods are quantitative and present concrete, statistical information when calculated and interpreted. Informal methods may include observation, interviews, incidents, stories, comments, letters, or impressions. Informal methods or qualitative measures can be significant when common themes or patterns begin to surface. This begins the synthesis process of deriving meaning from the information collected. Both formal and informal methods of collecting feedback are important as they relate to movement toward the desired results of the organization. Focusing on the feedback of a narrow perspective is unlikely to lead to a well-aligned system. A wide range of feedback sources combined with a synthesis of the information gathered has a greater potential of surfacing leverage points.

A proactive process of making informed decisions about adjustments in structures that guide us to our desired results is purposeful management. Using a variety of feedback mechanisms to gain the necessary information for making wise decisions is being "informed." When purposefully planned and used to guide the organization toward desired results, feedback becomes the essential mechanism for organizations striving for improvement.

64 ✧ **Structuring Schools for Success**

Suggested Procedure 1: Resources for Feedback Mechanisms

All stakeholders in an organization should be included as feedback mechanisms are planned and implemented. The following will provide the reader with ideas and examples for consideration. It is important that the school leaders plan the collection of feedback in order to get honest, valid information about the opinions and perceptions from a variety of viewpoints. Then, as patterns and common threads become evident, a plan for modifications, deletions, or additions in structure can be implemented. Sample feedback mechanisms are provided for gathering information from students, staff, and parents.

Students
    a. Beginning-of-the-year temperature check (students rate their first week of school on a scale from 1 to 10 and support their rating)
    b. Confidential surveys on topics
    c. Student committee discussions
    d. Lunch table opinion polls
    e. Data collected over time on numbers of participants in extracurricular activities
    f. Discipline referral data
    g. Standardized test scores
    h. Observational data on student behaviors before school, between classes, and after school
    i. Climate surveys
    j. Interviews
    k. Honor roll and improvement honor roll data

Staff
    a. Staff climate surveys
    b. Minutes of team meetings
    c. Administrative time needed by a staff member—quantity and nature of need
    d. Staff attendance records
    e. Instructional skill evaluations
    f. Administrative evaluations
    g. Professional-growth activities pursued by staff
    h. Observation of the use of free time by staff

i. Opinion polls
j. In-service workshops and planning meetings
k. Written notes and memos

Parents
a. Parent phone calls
b. Parent surveys
c. Parent organization meeting minutes (Parent-Teacher Association or PTA, Parent-Teacher Organization or PTO, etc.)
d. Parent seminars
e. Responses to questions in newsletters
f. Parent volunteers
g. Parent notes and letters
h. Parent meetings and interviews
i. Parents asked to review drafts of policy, communication, publications, and so on before final products are put in place
j. Attendance in evening seminars, meetings, workshops, open houses, and so on
k. Informal comments

With all of these samples of feedback mechanisms, it is crucial not to fall into the panic-and-respond mode when a concern surfaces. The importance of looking for patterns when collecting feedback is a necessary step when synthesizing both formal and informal methods of gathering information.

In the following example, feedback is used to increase the degree of understanding about a situation and to identify leverage through synthesis.

Suggested Procedure 2: An Example

> Situation: An administrator is faced with a school environment where there is a perception that students are ill-mannered, the detention room is always full, and there is a question of emotional safety on campus.
>
> Gathering feedback: The first thing that the administrator should do is check out the perception. Counting numbers of referrals and categorizing the nature of infractions,

interviewing students, observing behaviors during and between classes, discussing the topic during a student government meeting and checking parental impressions through conversations, parent meetings, and so on are all valid methods of collecting information about the concerns over school environment.

Determining leverage: A synthesis of the information gathered combined with existing knowledge about student needs and behaviors should follow the gathering of feedback. The synthesis should allow the administrator to identify the source(s) of the problems and the leverage actions that will be most likely to change the undesirable behaviors.

Return to gathering feedback

Structural Alignment

The alignment of structures begins with the clarification of desired results. Desired results range from the building of a shared vision for the whole organization (process described in chapter 4) to the identification of specific outcomes for each element of the organization. These goals are crucial structures. They reflect both purpose and standards for measurement of progress. They should serve as guideposts for all decisions and actions. Alignment of other structures in the organization is dependent on accuracy and specificity of desired results.

Prior to aligning structures, common understandings of the desired results should be verified. Time spent on the clarification of desired results is very worthwhile as it will facilitate the alignment of structures. Shared perceptions about the intention and meaning of the desired results will help staff members to more easily identify matches and mismatches with structures.

The first step to alignment is increasing the awareness of various types of structures that affect the results produced by a school. Organizational design includes a myriad of possibilities for grouping and scheduling of students and staff as well as a wide variety of roles. Policies, rules, guidelines, time lines, regulations, procedures, and so on affect thinking and behavior. Examples of practices range from the specific instructional strategies used in the classrooms to the behaviors exhibited in staff meetings. The mental models of students and staff are represented in each of the categories listed above. Recognizing the variety, complexity, and interrelationships of these structures can lead to the identification of leverage in making improvements.

Before structures can be altered to better fit the goals of an organization, it is necessary to increase awareness about the variety of structures that affect productivity.

Suggested Procedure 1: Identifying Structures

Step 1: Identify a change that is desired in the school. It might involve student behavior, student academic performance, staff communication, staff relationships, or other new programs or practices.

Step 2: Assign groups of staff members to list the various structures that will affect the implementation of the change.

Step 3: Have groups of staff members categorize the structures under the headings of organizational design, policies, practices, and mental models.

Step 4: Bring the groups together to report on their lists. It is likely that the lists will vary and that some discussion about interdependencies between the structures will have occurred. Encourage the continuation of that discussion. During this discussion, mental models about how the school operates will surface. It is important for staff members to compare assumptions about the effect of various structures. If consensus about the various interrelationships and their relative importance to the implementation of the change or goal can be reached, leverage can be more easily identified.

A second step to alignment is gathering feedback to determine the productivity of the existing structures. Examination of the structures in place in many schools is likely to result in some mismatches in purpose or in results produced. Studying the structures, evaluating the potential of each to produce the results desired, and working to bring about greater alignment can increase effectiveness. It is important to avoid immediate or massive changing of structures. Inconsistencies may reflect a need to reexamine the vision and purpose of the school. Clarifying intentions and aligning structures should be a recursive process that is accompanied by extensive dialogue that includes both analysis and synthesis. The complexity of the interrelationships should be considered. Acquiring a variety of perspectives on the situation decreases the likelihood of conclusions that disregard the "big picture." Small changes that appear to have great potential impact are the goal. It is better to take the time for a thorough study than to make the wrong changes too soon.

Suggested Procedure 2: Aligning Policies

Involve staff, students, and parents in a comparison of the policies, rules, guidelines, and so on that are described in the handbook with the goals of the school. This activity is most efficiently completed with a small group of representatives. The group can be assigned to study the entire handbook and to look for blatant inconsistencies as well as areas of ambiguity. Symbols (such as + and –) can be used to indicate the parts that are congruent with the goals of the school and for the parts that are inconsistent or misleading. The areas of concern should be carefully considered for change. The handbook may appear to represent only a small aspect of the school but the messages communicated affect all students. The conclusion of the group may be that the contents of the handbook are consistent with the goals of the school, but that the problem lies in the interpretation and execution of the rules and guidelines. If this is the case, the leverage may lie in dialogue about the use of the handbook or the meaning of the contents. Studying the handbook as a structure may be only the beginning of the process that will lead to improved alignment of other structures.

Suggested Procedure 3: Aligning Organizational Design

The organizational design should provide individual job descriptions and groupings that are likely to facilitate the production of desired results. In some schools, a coprincipalship may be more effective than a principal and an assistant principal. The custodial staff may work better with a leader assigned to make most decisions rather than waiting on approval from the principal. In other situations, the perspective of the principal is essential. Forming interdisciplinary teams of three teachers may make sense for one school, whereas teams of five are better for another.

For example, the makeup and scheduling of interdisciplinary teams should be based on the outcomes that are desired.

> Step 1: Ask staff members to list desired interdisciplinary outcomes on sheets of poster paper.
> Step 2: Have groups share their lists. Through dialogue and consensus, determine the goals of interdisciplinary instruction that can be supported by the whole group.
> Step 3: Give each group samples of various teaming configurations and instruct them to compare the abilities of certain groupings to produce desired outcomes. Tell them that they may also think of new configurations that are better.
> Step 4: Following the comparisons, discuss the conclusions. Use a consensus process to make decisions about the configuration that is most likely to produce desired results.

It should be noted that, once a particular configuration is put into place, it is important to "stick with it" long enough to study results. One school year is probably not enough time. If possible, results should be studied for 2 to 3 years while working on the abilities of the individuals in the groups to collaborate.

Suggested Procedure 4: Identifying Productive and Nonproductive Structures

Another activity can be conducted to take a wide look at organizational structures and the fit between those structures and the desired results of the school.

> Step 1: Assign staff members to job-alike groups.
> Step 2: Provide each group with lists of desired results and/or goals that are pertinent to their job descriptions. These

lists may include both whole school goals and goals specific to different areas.

Step 3: Assign each group to discuss the list of desired results to assure common understanding.

Step 4: Assign each group to list the structures that affect their ability to produce the results desired and to indicate the specific result(s) to which each structure is related. Instruct them to indicate a positive relationship with a plus sign (+) and a negative relationship with a minus sign (–). They may choose to use other symbols or a diagram to represent the interrelationships that also exist.

Step 5: Assign each group to study the result lists and indications of relationships. Ask them to discuss potential changes.

Step 6: Using a consensus process, assign each group to determine an area of leverage, a structural change that is most likely to produce positive results. Encourage them to think of small changes or large changes in small steps. They should also think about potential short- and long-term effects in their area as well as other areas.

Step 7: Following appropriate procedures for the situation, assist each group in following through with a plan of the desired changes. They should receive guidance in making plans for necessary communication, inclusion of other individuals or groups, consideration of potential problems, and so on.

Suggested Procedure 5: Aligning Mental Models

The ability of any individual or group to produce desired results depends greatly on their beliefs, assumptions, past experiences, and so on. These factors influence behavior, regardless of the other structures that exist in the organization. In schools, we have often changed the expectations or the organizational design with little or no regard for existing attitudes or skills. For example, the following scenarios may be familiar:

- If learning outcomes have changed to involve higher-order thinking skills, some changes in beliefs about instructional strategies will be necessary.
- If special-needs students are to be included in all classes, some changes in attitudes about student learning will be necessary.
- If integrated curriculum is a goal, the value of collaboration will have to be demonstrated.
- If an analysis of current conditions results in a concern over staff abilities to communicate, a lesson in dialogue may be necessary.

It is best to begin with simple, low-risk tasks such as those described in chapter 2. Following a dialogue practice session with a carefully chosen topic, staff members should be assigned to compare similarities and differences that became apparent and to describe the potential effects of those differences on the ability to achieve the vision of the school.

Step 1: Review the rules of dialogue.

Step 2: Assign the dialogue topic. Example: Student will have opportunities to apply learning to real-world situations.

Step 3: Assign small groups to engage in dialogue about the topic. What types of activities are consistent with this goal? What levels of thinking are expected? What outcomes are expected? What types of assessment are applicable? How often should such strategies be used?

Step 4: Assign the small groups to identify similarities and differences in the activities, strategies, and outcomes that are described.

Step 5: Assign the small groups to list the variety of results that might be produced by the differences in thinking about the goal.

Step 6: Assign the small groups to achieve consensus about a definition of strategies that are consistent with the goal and to write a statement that includes guidelines for teaching that is aimed at achieving the goal.

Step 7: Have small groups report to the whole group. Work with the whole group to build consensus about the statement that best fits the needs of the whole school.

Engaging in dialogue about possible differences of opinion helps staff members to be more aware of their own personal thinking and assumptions and to better understand the differences that may exist in the thinking and assumptions of others. Personal thinking can change based on this awareness. In addition, staff members can become increasingly cognizant of the importance of consistent thinking and behavior for the purpose of achieving greater potential to achieve results.

The process of alignment begins with clarifying desired results and requires a deep respect for the power of various structures to affect our ability to produce those results. Although we are often aware that some aspects of our system are not conducive to producing desired results, analyzing and aligning structures is not a common practice. The complexity of the process involved and the time required are often deterrents to a thorough study of how a school works. "Unfortunately, many of the most vexing problems confronting managers and corporations today are caused by a web of tightly interconnected circular relationships" (Goodman, 1991, p. 3). Beginning the process with one aspect of the system and practicing the habits of considering interrelationships and searching for leverage will most often bring about very satisfying results. Individuals involved in such a process can be empowered by inclusion in the feedback about and assessment of the structures in a system. The results can be greater personal and group responsibility for producing desired results. The structures of the system can no longer be excuses for lack of ownership in the change process. We must see ourselves as influential managers of a system that is complex and ever changing. Through new awareness and skills, we can make adjustments that will increase the effectiveness of each subsystem in a school and of the school as a whole.

Key Terms and Concepts

Analysis. The separating of any entity into its constituent elements.

Clarification. The process of using dialogue, description, images, and other strategies to increase the understanding of a vision, desired results, or any other aspects of the organization.

Feedback. Information about the results that our behavior and decisions are producing.

Interdependent relationships. Circular, mutually causative relationships.

Leverage. The concept of identifying and taking actions that are most likely to produce the results desired.

Participatory management. An organizational system in which many staff members have opportunities to participate in decision making, planning, management, and so on. This concept could be a part of other management models.

Shared vision. A governing force guiding each member of the organization, as measured by the consistency of the beliefs, values, and assumptions with the everyday decisions and behaviors of the members.

Synthesis. The combining of separate parts or elements to form a whole.

System dynamics. A field of study that uses methodologies for the purpose of understanding feedback, complexity, interdependence, and the process of change.

Systems thinking. "An emerging paradigm from the field of system dynamics—the study of time-varying systems, their internal structures, their cause and effect and feedback relationships, and the communications and energy flows within those structures" (Draper, 1991).

TQM. Total Quality Management.

Sources

Brown, G. S. (1990). *The genesis of the Systems Thinking Program at the Orange Grove Middle School.* Tucson, AZ: Systems Thinking Project.

Costa, A. (1989). *The art of cognitive coaching.* Sacramento, CA: The Institute For Intelligent Behavior.

Draper, F. (1991, April). *Integrating systems thinking and simulation into the eighth grade science curriculum.* Paper presented at the annual meeting of the American Educational Research Association, Chicago, IL.

Goodman, M. (1991). Systems thinking as a language. *The Systems Thinker, 2*(3), 3-4.

Recommended Literature

Forrester, J. W. (1971). Counterintuitive behavior of social systems. *Technology Review, 73*(3), 53-68.

Forrester, J. W. (1991). System dynamics—Adding structure and relevance to precollege education. In K. R. Manning (Ed.), *MIT—Shaping the future* (pp. 1-16). Cambridge, MA: MIT Press.

Lyneis, J. M. (1980). *Corporate planning and policy design: A system dynamics approach.* Cambridge, MA: Productivity Press.

Richardson, G. P. (1991). *Feedback thought in social science and systems theory.* Philadelphia: University of Pennsylvania Press.

Walton, M. (1986). *The Deming management method.* New York: G. P. Putman.

✧ 6 ✧

Using Support Structures Outside of the School

The Need for Outside Support Structures

In previous chapters, the need to develop consistent thinking and behaviors on the part of the school staff were discussed. However, a school does not exist in isolation. Other entities of the district, the community, and the world at large can affect and assist in the production of desired results. Individuals and groups from a particular school can be surprised or disappointed about the lack of alignment between their goals and the goals of other groups. Failure to maintain a fit between school plans and the plans of other potential support groups can result in major roadblocks to progress. Inclusion of other groups in initial steps and continued communication about next steps help to build a high-level awareness of interdependence. Potential resources and assistance may surface when feedback and involvement are made welcome.

The District

Understanding and support from the central office administration and from other schools is a major factor in producing the desired outcomes of the school. In the initial stages of building a shared school vision, it is important to compare the school goals that are evolving with the vision and the goals of the school

76 ❖ **Structuring Schools for Success**

district and of the other schools. Just as communication and collaboration are important within the school, these practices are important with other aspects of the school system.

Suggested Procedure: Comparing Vision Statements With District Mission Statements or Goals

During the building and clarifying of a shared vision, the identification of specific desired results, and the alignment of structures, examples of related information from the central office and from other schools should be used.

> Step 1: Assign small groups of staff members to compare a set of school vision statements with the district mission statement or goals. Each group will have a different set. The number of statements in each set will depend on the total number to be divided among the groups.
> Step 2: Assign each group to answer the following questions:
> a. Does each vision statement support the district mission statement or goals?
> b. Does each statement appear to represent a clarification or a more specific aspect of the district mission statement or goals?
> c. If a statement does not support or clarify the district mission statement or goals, is there another reasonable connection?
> d. Is there a conflict between the outcomes represented by any vision statement and the district mission statement or goals?
> Step 3: Bring the groups together for a report on their comparisons.
> Step 4: If any apparent conflicts are identified, make a plan for next steps.
> a. Is it possible that more information is needed? Discussion with central office representatives might result in different interpretations of the mission or goal statements or a desire to adjust the mission statement or goals.

b. Is it possible to adjust the school vision statement to achieve greater alignment?

Step 5: If a school vision statement does not support or clarify the mission statement or goals but also does not seem to conflict, determine whether retention of the school vision statement would be advisable.

   a. Is it possible that the school vision statement could be an appropriate school outcome and is simply not a part of a more general district mission statement or goals?

   b. Is it necessary to acquire approval for the school vision statements that are not obviously connected to the district mission statement or goals?

Step 6: Depending on the answers to the questions above, proceed as necessary.

The procedure described above can be used as a way to ensure alignment while the vision and desired results are being clarified. Involvement of representatives from the central office or from other schools during earlier stages of personal-vision activities and/or shared-vision activities is another alternative. Asking individuals from other aspects of the school vision to share in these activities may result in support and understanding from the beginning and may encourage similar activities in other parts of the system. However, contributing time and efforts to the work of a school in which one does not work may not be feasible. If this is true, the procedure suggested is the best alternative.

The Community

Parents and other community members are important stakeholders in the vision and desired results of a school. In many ways, the support and understanding of the parents is as important as the commitment and the follow-through of the staff. Because members of the community are often asked to demonstrate support through their votes, their attitudes about the school can also influence success.

Involvement of representatives from parent and community groups in both personal visioning and development of a shared vision is wise and appropriate. The parents and community members who are involved should be included as equal participants in the process in order to validate the importance of their opinions. It is important to seek individuals who represent a variety of perspectives on the district. Although it may not be possible to represent all views, attempts should be made to encourage participation from a spectrum of viewpoints.

- Parents of students from different grade levels
- Parents who have only one child in school
- Parents who have several students in school
- Parents who have exhibited support in other instances
- Parents who may have raised questions
- Community members who are retired
- Community members whose children have graduated
- Community members who have no children
- Community members who work in the area
- Community members who work outside of the area

In addition to involvement in the process, consistent communication about the vision and desired results of the school continues to be important. The following vehicles for communication can be used:

- Newsletters
- Parent meetings or open houses
- Fliers sent home with students
- Before-school letters to parents
- Homeowner association meetings
- Area newspaper articles
- Parent seminars on specific aspects of the vision
- Discussions lead by parent group representatives

Suggested Procedures: Involving Parents

Parent groups such as PTA, PTO, booster clubs, and so on should be familiar with the vision and desired results of the school. Such groups can be involved in two ways:

1. Using Existing Parent Groups for Alignment
   a. Step 1: Share information about the vision and desired results with the chosen group.
   b. Step 2: Ask the group to determine the ways in which the goals of the group can be aligned with the vision of the school.
   c. Step 3: Ask the group to determine ways in which the activities and operations of the group can be aligned with the desired results.
2. Using Parents for Feedback
   a. Step 1: Share information about the vision and desired results with all parents through a newsletter article.
   b. Step 2: Ask parents to respond to the article by assessing the degree to which desired results are being produced through the use of a rating scale (e.g., 5 = *high satisfaction* to 1 = *low satisfaction*). Or ask parents to respond to the article by indicating the 10 most important desired results and adding any desired results that they believe should be addressed.
   c. Step 3: Follow up on the results of the type of feedback chosen by studying the results and determining what changes, if any, might be necessary.

Although extensive formal communication is helpful, the most powerful influences are the reports of students. When the vision and the desired results successfully serve the needs of students, they take positive reports to parents. The resulting parent satisfaction affects the attitudes of new parents and other members of the community. An important aspect of student reports to parents is the degree to which students understand the vision and the desired results of the school. Students can be involved in the process of building a shared vision. Depending on their ages, students can express needs and personal visions for their education. In later stages, student feedback about the achievement of desired outcomes is useful. This feedback can be acquired in periodic meetings with representative groups or surveys of all students. It can also happen on a regular basis in classrooms and other student activities. The more that students understand the purpose of the activities in which they are involved, the better they are able to communicate that purpose to their parents.

Other Possibilities

Business partnerships are a growing trend in education and promise great potential for reciprocal benefits. A proponent of business partnerships, Bob Stensland of Portland (Oregon), suggests that these partnerships be viewed not as relationships between institutions but relationships between individuals. This view was shared during a presentation at the 1993 Network for Improving Educational Thinking Conference in Tucson, Arizona. Educators approaching a representative from the business world should be prepared to discuss the possible value of working together. Anticipation of the possible perceptions that a businessperson might have of education or of an educator's reason for seeking a partnership is helpful. Members of the business world often assume that educators do not want input and refuse accountability. Their views have been affected by their own educational experiences and by current negative publicity about education. In conference presentations, Jill Kirk, vice president of human relations and director of Tektronix, Inc. in Beaverton, Oregon, has characterized educators as often assuming that businesspeople want only to interfere in their professional arena and that they are only interested in schools producing good workers. It is important to discuss these assumptions and to work toward a common set of goals and a mutually beneficial plan. The reality is that there is increasing congruence between business and education objectives. Both are interested in accountability, relevant educational experiences, critical thinking, cooperative work, and lifelong learning (The Secretary's Commission on Achieving Necessary Skills [SCANS], 1992). We must build on these congruent goals and work toward common visions if we hope to maximize the potential of improving education.

Another type of partnership is the concept of the citizen champion. In every community, there are individuals who do not have students in school but who possess a great interest in helping educators. These individuals may work in the community or they may be retired. In either case, it is necessary to invite them into the school to increase their understanding of how schools work and to identify possible connections between the school and their areas of expertise and experience. Because educators are often face-to-face with a great number of challenges and responsibilities, the perspective of a noneducator can often help them to stand back and to look at a situation from a different perspective or to get a better understanding of the big picture.

Example

Dr. Gordon Brown, a retired dean of the engineering school at the Massachusetts Institute of Technology (MIT), is a resident of the Catalina Foothills community. Dr. Brown expressed an interest in the use of laser disc technology in the Orange Grove science classes. After visiting the classes and talking with the teachers, he shared information about a concept that could possibly be used in science instruction. Through his relationships with individuals involved in the field of system dynamics, he was able to make arrangements for staff training. His continued work with the school has produced many additional resources including grant funding and mentoring by experts. An invaluable fringe benefit of this relationship has been the constant reminder from a person outside of the school of a more global view.

In every community, there is potential for identifying citizen champions. It is essential for schools to take the lead in seeking these relationships. The following suggested procedure may help in the identification of potential partnerships.

Suggested Procedure: Identifying Potential Partnerships

Step 1: Engage in discussions about the idea of involving community members as partners in the school. Explain the purpose of the partnership. Be sure to reinforce the value of sharing expertise and experience. Although financial resources may be a by-product of the relationship, this should not be the main motivation for the partnership.

Step 2: Contact potential citizen champions. Invite them to your school. Prior to the visit, try to determine the area of schools that is of most interest to them. Identify ways in which the school might be of service to individuals. Increased understanding might be the initial goal.

Step 3: Nurture the relationship. Because this concept is not commonly practiced, it may take some time to develop trust and understanding.

Misconceptions about schools and dissatisfaction about results being produced are often a result of lack of information or understanding. We cannot ignore the opinions of community members nor should we underestimate the potential value of their assistance and support.

Key Terms and Concepts

Analysis. The separating of any entity into its constituent elements.

Business partnerships. Relationships in which businesses and schools work out an agreement for mutually beneficial goods and/or services. These agreements range from speakers in classes to the full-time loan of personnel. In some cases, they involve financing of a project or provision of training.

Citizen champion. An individual who chooses to develop a working relationship with a school. The relationship might include mentoring or training. The perspectives gained from working with a person who is not an educator can be very beneficial.

Clarification. The process of using dialogue, description, images, and other strategies to increase the understanding of a vision, desired results, or any other aspect of an organization.

Feedback. Information about the results that our behavior and decisions are producing.

Interdependent relationships. Circular, mutually causative relationships.

Leverage. The concept of identifying and taking actions that are most likely to produce the results desired.

Participatory management. An organizational system in which many staff members have opportunities to participate in decision making, planning, management, and so on. This concept could be a part of other management models.

Shared vision. A governing force guiding each member of the organization, as measured by the consistency of the beliefs, values, and assumptions with the everyday decisions and behaviors of the members.

Synthesis. The combining of separate parts or elements to form a whole.

System dynamics. A field of study that uses methodologies for the purpose of understanding feedback, complexity, interdependence, and the process of change.

Systems thinking. "An emerging paradigm from the field of system dynamics—the study of time-varying systems, their internal structures, their cause and effect and feedback relationships, and the communications and energy flows within those structures" (Draper, 1991).

TQM. Total Quality Management.

Sources

Draper, F. (1991, April). *Integrating systems thinking and simulation into the eighth grade science curriculum.* Paper presented at the annual meeting of the American Educational Research Association, Chicago, IL.

The Secretary's Commission on Achieving Necessary Skills (SCANS). (1992). *What work requires of schools.* Washington, DC: Department of Labor.

✧ 7 ✧

Visualizing Next Steps

Asking Essential Questions

The importance of asking questions should not be underestimated. Gaining a variety of perspectives by asking questions can help shape an individual's understanding and is essential to the interdependent nature of the school organization. It is recognized that many questions have been left unanswered in this book. This is because there are no mysterious insights or secret formulas that are guaranteed to work in any organization. It is important to understand that successful solutions to problems in one school setting will not likely produce the same results in another setting, no matter how similar. No two schools are exactly alike. Specific "how to's" become contrary to the belief that it is essential to make decisions based on the special conditions and structures of the organization at hand.

As organizational leaders make plans, the following commonly asked questions may help to provide a foundation for starting points. They should begin to help address the familiar questions: "Where do we start?" or "What should I do first?" Thinking about what information individuals in the organization may need to answer the following questions will help formulate a beginning:

- What is the shared vision of our school and who should be a part of developing and clarifying it?
- What results do we want our school to produce? For students? For staff? For parents? For community?

- What are the success indicators that demonstrate quality in our school?
- What skills and abilities should students demonstrate as adult citizens?
- Are these skills and abilities modeled for students by staff members on a regular basis? How?
- What role does each staff member play in working toward the desired results of the organization?

The answers to these questions are not simple. They involve the synthesis of the diverse perspectives and viewpoints of the various stakeholders of the organization. This can provide the starting point for examining the current conditions existing in the organization and help clarify the direction in which the organization is headed.

Successive Approximation

Suffice it to say that the more one learns, the more one realizes how much is truly unknown or misunderstood. The quest for understanding then becomes an ongoing process of "successive approximation." A prominent businessman, Jim Waters, president of the Waters Foundation, is a proponent of this strategy to help organizations mature and develop. It is much like taking small steps, moving toward a final destination or goal by carefully evaluating each step of the way. This approach requires patience, which is a challenge in times when there are pressures to produce immediate, noticeable results in improving education. Long-term, significant improvements take time and will not be accomplished as a result of quick fixes or snap decisions.

A recursive process of repetitive steps enables the educational leader to effectively engage in significant, yet gradual organizational development. As already explained and illustrated through many of the previously described activities labeled "suggested procedures," a framework for the process may include the following:

- Assessing and analyzing the current conditions

- Determining leverage
- Making a decision
- Synthesizing feedback
- Repeating the process

Although this process may seem time intensive, much joy can be realized as organizations reach increasingly sophisticated levels of development. The attainment of these levels can be recognized and celebrated by members and can also be observable by individuals who are not part of the organization. This validation for the growth and development of individuals, and the organization as a whole, is one of the most exciting aspects of being an educational leader.

Responses and Responsibilities

When responding to questions, it is important to understand the needs of all learners. Needs are complex, as illustrated by the master teacher who grapples with the questions: "Is it best to provide learners with the answers to their questions?" or "Is it advantageous to teach learners strategies to help them seek and develop their own answers to questions or solutions to problems?" As school organizations develop and mature, individuals within the organization grow as learners who accept and value personal responsibility for responding to questions by seeking various possibilities.

When members of schools feel empowered as essential, needed contributors to the success of the organization, the extent to which individuals take personal responsibility for the achievement of desired results increases. Individuals tend to assume personal responsibility when certain conditions exist. The following organizational values and beliefs are desirable in building these conditions:

- *All members* of the school staff should be involved with organizational development activities such as skill development training, shared-vision and desired-results clarification. "Every staff member contributes to the success of a school."

- Labels and titles should be carefully chosen and used—that is, using the label *staff* instead of *faculty* because faculty suggests *only* teaching personnel. "Titles, names, and labels should be inclusive, validating, and respectful."
- Model the behaviors expected of all staff members. "Walk the talk and practice what you preach."
- Staff members should feel safe in tactfully expressing concerns, inconsistencies, and sensitive issues. "You can't work to improve situations you don't know anything about."

It is believed that it is the responsibility of the educational leader to work toward the conditions described above. When things go differently than planned, a mature organization minimizes the need to blame. Blame is unproductive, works against individuals developing personal responsibility, and fractures the organization. When unpredicted events occur, the following questions may help individuals avoid blaming:

- What could I have done differently that would have minimized this condition?
- What can I do to help to ensure that this will not happen again?
- What support will I need to help me with my efforts?

Notice that all of the proposed questions are asked in the first person. By turning the responsibility inward, the tendency to blame other people or other things becomes minimized. When all members of an organization work to see problems in this light, the problems become learning opportunities and not setbacks.

Suggested Procedure: Planning for Organizational Development

The following goals are recommended as leaders plan a step-by-step process for organizational development. These conditions are broad, yet basic in creating schools that will most likely meet the needs of students, staff, and community. Organizations should strive to develop the following:

- Students, staff, and community who see themselves as learners and take personal responsibility for this role
- An organization that focuses on the learning needs of all students, staff, and community
- Environments where a variety of perspectives are valued
- Environments where innovations thrive because risk taking is encouraged

Written from a practitioner's view, concepts, processes, and sequences of procedures for developing effective organizations have been discussed and illustrated in this book. It is the sincere hope that the ideas presented in this book act as catalysts to the thoughtful decision making and planning of educational leaders as they work to improve schools. The suggested procedures should not be viewed as the only methods for achieving a thriving, productive organization. Individuals are encouraged to modify and adjust suggested procedures and practices and to carefully plan the next best steps for the effective organizational development of their schools.

If you are thinking a year ahead, sow seed.
If you are thinking ten years ahead, plant a tree.
If you are thinking one hundred years ahead, educate the people.

(CHINESE POET, 500 B.C.)

Key Terms and Concepts

Successive approximation. Moving closer and closer to a desired result or goal by going through a process of taking small steps, assessing, and making plans for future steps.

Recommended Literature

Bridges, W. (1991). *Managing transitions—Making the most of change.* Reading, MA: Addison-Wesley.

Planning and Troubleshooting Guide

Analyzing the School Organization

Behaviors of staff are not aligned with desired results	59-60
How can needed changes be identified?	67-73
Need feedback to increase perspectives and understanding	63-64
Need to determine most effective changes to make	61-62
Perceptions of student behavior are negative	67-68
Structures or organization need alignment	56-57
System cannot deal with interdependent relationships	4-5
What feedback mechanisms are available?	64-65

Changing Paradigms

Changing from linear thinking is difficult	9-10
Changing old paradigms is difficult	41-44
Dependence on a hierarchical system needs changing	33-34
Existing paradigms are hidden and unexamined	36-41
Interdependence is not understood or appreciated	2-13
Staff is unaware of existing paradigms or mental models	2-3
Staff is unaware of interdependent relationships in schools	4-5
Staff tends to operate in isolation	2-3
Systems need manageable subsystems	4-6

Developing Communication Skills

Collaboration is hindered by lack of communication skills	24-28
Discussion often means a win-lose result	17-20
Personal responsibility for actions is lacking	6-8
Staff members do not feel a sense of community	28-31
Staff members need practice in group decision making	20-22
Stress causes communication problems	22-24

Developing Support Structures Outside the School

Community members do not feel ownership in program	77-79
District understanding and support is needed	75-77
Potential advocates are underused	80-82

Determining Desired Results

How do we combine personal visions into shared vision?	49-51
How do we keep the shared vision current and dynamic?	51-53
What exactly are we trying to accomplish?	46-47
What personal visions does each staff member possess?	47-48
What specific results should be measured?	53-56

Helpful Hints for Success

Big plans often lead to big mistakes	5
Differences in beliefs present problems	39
Lack of understanding of differences hinders progress	11
Resources are needed to understand interdependence	6
Staff members are reluctant to share personal opinions	41
Staff members are uncomfortable with group activities	24
Time for staff development is lacking	30

Planning and Troubleshooting Guide ✧ 91

Risk Factors to Be Considered

Avoid putting staff members in defensive positions	28
Developing trust and personal responsibility is crucial	60
Large-group presentations are threatening	50
Learning about personal habits is difficult	24
Mental models change slowly	40
Narrative descriptions of visions should be avoided at first	48
Staff members seek safety in linear thinking	11
Trust necessary for teamwork needs development	27

Suggested Procedures

Addressing interdependencies	4
Aligning behaviors	59
Aligning mental models	71
Aligning organizational design	69
Aligning policies	68
Asking the big questions	10
Assigning goal-oriented team tasks	26
Building a goal-oriented team	26, 27
Clarifying shared vision	52
Communication role play	20
Deriving desired results	55
Designing staff development	13
Developing a professional growth process	29
Developing advocacies and partnerships	81
Developing awareness of mental models	37
Developing community support	78
Developing district support	76
Developing personal visions	48
Developing shared vision	50
Examining mental models	36-39
Identifying productive and nonproductive structures	70
Identifying structures	67
Increasing effectiveness and efficiency	4
Practice in open-mindedness	7

Practicing a new view	9
Practicing team decision making	26
Resources for feedback mechanisms	64, 66
Revisiting the vision	54
Testing assumptions	42
Understanding communication under stress	22

371.2 SCHEETZ, MARY
SCH22S STRUCTURING
SCHOOLS FOR
SUCCESS.
10/20/95 C. 1 ERL

**MADISON METROPOLITAN SCHOOL DISTRICT
LIBRARY MEDIA CENTER**